WELCOME

Hello, and welcome to Improve Your Golf. Over the 20 years I've been a PGA professional, the game of golf has evolved immensely – and that includes the way it's been taught.

Every monthly golf magazine runs glossy tutorials that have – over time – been getting progressively more technical, with the basic fundamentals increasingly buried beneath a pile of confusing technical jargon.

This is ironic because, in the world of golf tuition, the fundamentals are the one thing about the game that haven't changed; learning how to hold the club properly, how to stand to the ball and the basic swing transitions. Our goal with this guide is to de-clutter these fashionable, over-written technical tutorials and provide you with a clear, simple and pictorial overview of how to get the

fundamentals right. With our PGA pro qualified instructors – and a little help from Ryder Cup legend Ian Poulter – we hope you enjoy getting back-to-basics.

But it's not just tuition we've lined up for you; inside you'll find guides to: the best golfing breaks (both UK and abroad), the major tournaments of the golfing calendar, custom fitting and even the junior golfing scene.

We hope this core-skills approach will help you develop your enjoyment of this beautiful – if sometimes confusing – game, and please don't forget to flip over and take a look at our ultimate guide to this year's golfing equipment.

Enjoy!

Danny Poulter, PGA Professional

IMPROVE YOUR
GOLF

TUTORIALS

44

58

IAN POULTER
HOLING OUT MASTERCLASS

134

PLAYING THE GAME

77

66

100

SCOTTSDALE TR

WE'VE REVOLUTIONISED THE PUTTER. AGAIN.

VARIABLE DEPTH GROOVES

TRUE ROLL INSERT

CUSTOM ENGINEERED TO CREATE CONSISTENT BALL SPEEDS ACROSS THE FACE. DEEPER GROOVES IN THE MIDDLE, SHALLOWER TOWARD THE PERIMETER.

UNMATCHED DISTANCE CONTROL

AN INDUSTRY-FIRST INNOVATION, THE VARIABLE DEPTH GROOVE INSERT PROVIDES FORGIVENESS ACROSS THE FACE. THAT MEANS BETTER DISTANCE CONTROL, WHICH MEANS FEWER PUTTS.

38"

31"

ADJUSTABLE SHAFT LENGTH

WE'VE ELEVATED PUTTER FITTING BY BRINGING YOU A PUTTER SHAFT THAT ADJUSTS WITHIN A SEVEN-INCH RANGE TO BRING YOU THE MOST PRECISE FIT IN GOLF. TOGETHER WITH OUR FIT FOR STROKE™ CONCEPT AND THE iPING® PUTTER APP, PUTTER FITTING HAS NEVER BEEN SO EASY AND EFFECTIVE.

The Scottsdale® TR™ putter's new insert has consistency down to a science. Its variable depth grooves, machined into an aerospace grade 6061 aluminium insert, create unmatched distance control. Whether you hit it dead centre or toward the heel or toe, your putts travel nearly the same distance. Add even more consistency with an adjustable shaft (optional) in one of 12 models. Visit a PING® Fitting Specialist or ping.com.

CONTENTS

THE WORLD OF GOLF

IMPROVE YOUR GOLF

Editorial
Writer Danny Poulter
Photography Danny Bird
Hair & Make-up Katharina Sherman
Contributors Tommy Melville, Sam Smith, Joe Reemer
Art Editor Rob Callaghan
Creative Retouching Reprographics Jan Cihak (Tapestry)
Digital Production Manager Nicky Baker

Management
MagBook Publisher Dharmesh Mistry
Production Director Robin Ryan
MagBook Advertising Director Katie Wood
(katie_wood@dennis.co.uk)
MagBook Account Executive Emma D'Arcy
MD of Advertising Julian Lloyd-Evans
Newstrade Director David Barker
MD of Enterprise Director Martin Belson
Chief Financial Officer Brett Reynolds
Group Finance Director Ian Leggett
Chief Executive James Tye
Chairman Felix Dennis

Dennis Publishing would like to thank the following people for making this MagBook possible: Ian Poulter. Sam Smith and Rob Leonard (PGA professionals at The Bedford Golf Club and Harpenden Common Golf Club respectively), Puma, Nike and IJP Design (who provided the apparel for our tutorial shoot), www.greatgolfdestinations.co.uk, Virgin Atlantic, The Emirates Golf Club and The Marriott Courtyard Dubai.

Improve Your Golf
ISBN 1–78106–133–5

Licensing & Liability

To license this product, please contact Carlotta Seratoni on +44 (0) 20 7907 6550, or email carlotta_serantoni@dennis.co.uk. To syndicate content from this product please contact Anj Dosaj Halai on +44(0) 20 7907 6132 or email anj_dosaj-halai@dennis.co.uk

PUT YOUR OWN SWING ON THINGS

KEEP YOUR HEAD STILL, HIPS ALIGNED AND SOME OTHER STUFF. THERE'S
THE TYPICAL WAY OF DOING THINGS, AND THEN THERE'S BUBBA'S WAY.

OAKLEY GOLF APPAREL
+ BUBBA WATSON

BEYOND REASON | OAKLEY

THE TUTORIALS

HOW TO
HOLD

This is the most important part of the whole golf swing, as your hands are the only part of your body connected to the club, and the correct grip allows your hands to move correctly.

When getting to know the grip it is important you understand the pressure with which you hold the club is crucial. If you grip the club too tightly you run the risk of locking your wrist and forearms, stopping you from being able to rotate and hinge your wrists. Over-gripping will make your swing wooden and rigid, which is to be avoided at all costs.

There are three main grips taught, and all of them are correct. Choosing which grip to use depends a lot on both the size of your hands and your physical strength.

THE THREE GRIPS ARE KNOWN AS THE FOLLOWING

- **Baseball Grip** (10 Finger Grip)
- **Vardon Grip** (Overlapping Grip)
- **Interlocking Grip**

We will go through each of these in turn, showing you how to apply each to the club. This is where we will also start developing your routine, and good grip habits form a crucial basis from which to develop the rest of your technique.

BASEBALL GRIP

This is normally taught to junior golfers, as it gives them a little more control until they develop more strength in their hands and forearms. As they get stronger they will quickly move onto the Vardon or Interlocking grips.

This grip is the easiest to learn, but similar principles apply to the Vardon and Interlocking grips, and two knuckles should be visible on the left hand, with one and a half visible on the right hand. There is no interlocking or overlapping of the fingers, and all ten fingers hold the club.

KEY DO AND DON'T

Do lock your arms, but don't hold too tight – imagine the pressure you need to hold a tube of toothpaste without squeezing any paste out

REMEMBER

The distance between the little finger of your left hand (assuming you're right handed) and the very end (or butt) of the club should be about an inch

SWING THOUGHT

Maintain a constant pressure on the grip throughout the swing

HOW IMPORTANT

Every time you hit a ball, practise reapplying the hold

TOP TIP

Ensure your hands are in the right position by checking a 'V' is formed by the forefinger and thumb of your right hand

WEATHER CONSIDERATIONS

Make sure grips and gloves are as dry as possible in adverse weather

You also need to understand that your hands will always return to their natural position on the club when impacting the ball. As you can see from the above picture, two knuckles are visible on each hand.

Holding the club correctly during the swing, in the natural position, will greatly increase the chances of you delivering the club to the ball on line and at your target.

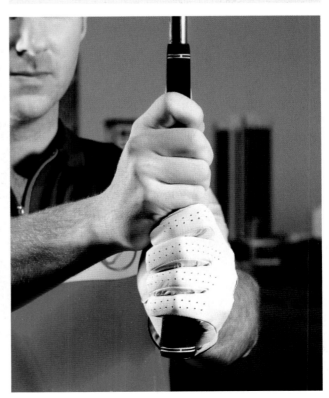

VARDON GRIP

This is the most popular grip, used by around 65% of golfers. It was invented, and first used, by Harry Vardon in the early 1900s, and has been mastered to great effect by many of the sport's greats.

For us, this is best grip. Not only does it force the hands to work together, but it also allows the wrists complete control of the club during the swing.

1 With the fingers of your left hand pointing towards the ground, rest the grip across the middle joint of your index finger, as shown right.

2 Next, carefully wrap the left hand onto the grip by placing the left thumb just right of the grip's centre. From the front you should now have two knuckles showing, with the heel of your hand resting along the grip.

This should also now create a 'V' between your thumb and forefinger, pointing towards your chin and right shoulder.

3 We are now going to place your right hand on the grip. Start by lifting the club vertically in front of you. Shape the tips of your fingers into a 'C' and slide them down the underside of the grip until they meet your left hand. Rest the little finger of your right hand in the groove between your left hand's index and middle finger. Now wrap your right hand's fingers onto the club, with your index finger flexed to support the back of the club while your thumb is placed to the left side of the grip, forming a 'V' that should match that of the left hand.

You should find that you have hidden the thumb of your left hand, and that it is running along the lifeline of your right hand.

Both palms should now be facing each other, with pressure distributed equally between them. Looking down at your hands, you should be able to see at least two knuckles on your left hand and one and a half knuckles on your right hand.

INTERLOCKING GRIP

4/5 Tiger Woods, the best golfer in the world, has used this grip throughout his glittering career, but these days it is usually taught to individuals lacking a little strength in the hands and wrist – something Tiger certainly isn't.

Applying the grip to the club follows a similar procedure as the Vardon grip above, with the small change that you should completely interlock the little finger of your right hand with the index finger of your left.

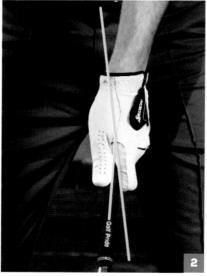
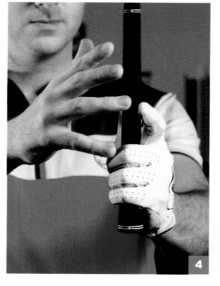

HOW TO
STAND

The stance is all about getting the feet placed comfortably and aligned parallel to your Ball to Target Line (more of which on page 26).

We are now going to start building a pre-shot routine that will help you into the correct position every time. Here we look at the basic stance, but will discuss stances for each particular shot in the later sections.

Simply place your feet shoulder width apart with the tips of your toes an equal distance away from the Body to Target Line.

1

KEY DO AND DON'T

Do be comfortable. You must always feel relaxed before taking your shot. Never rush your setup

TOP TIP

Make sure your toes are an equal distance from the Body to Target line, because if the feet are not in line, the rest of your body won't be either

WIND

Widen your stance slightly (a couple of inches) to make sure you create a sturdy base

2 You must make sure that your stance is not too wide (above left) as this may greatly reduce the amount you can turn your shoulders and body, causing a wooden swing. If your stance is too narrow (above right) it causes poor balance and can make your shoulder and hip movements uncontrolled and out of sync. We are looking to create a well-balanced and athletic position so that you are in total control when you start swinging the club.

THE CORRECT
POSTURE

Posture and body alignment are crucial components in the fragile collection of elements that make up the swing. A careful setup routine will help you get them right every time.

HERE IS A VERY SIMPLE **FOUR POINT PLAN TO** HELP YOU PERFECT YOUR POSTURE.

Standing straight, place your feet shoulder width apart.

Place a club across your hips and bend over it until you feel you are loosing your balance forward.

Flex your knees forward slightly to regain your balance and let your arms hang naturally in front you. Take your grip.

To make sure you're not standing too close to the ball, you need to be able pass an open-handed palm between the butt end of the club and yourself.

Once in the correct position, you should feel that your weight is evenly distributed and positioned towards the balls of your feet. If your weight is on your heels it will make swinging the club correctly more difficult, and will restrict your hips and shoulders from rotating properly. This will also cause a bending of your back, which is called stooping - something that must be avoided.

KEY DO AND DON'T

Don't stoop. Do make sure there is clear definition in your spine angle If you have a full-length mirror, practise in front of it whenever you can

REMEMBER

Your weight should always be positioned towards the balls of your feet

SWING THOUGHT

Balance is key, make sure you're in balance as this will mean that you're fully in control of your swing

TOP TIP

Correct posture is very hard to get right, a simple hour-long lesson with your PGA pro should help you iron out any posture issues

WIND

Aside from your feet, which should widen a little, your posture should stay the same whatever

Maintaining the angles shown in pictures 3 and 4 will lead to a tighter coil and a stronger position at the top of the swing, as Justin Rose shows here

Good posture puts your body in a natural position and creates what we like to call an athletic position. If you look at golfers on the TV you will be able to see that even though they all swing the club slightly differently, they all have a good posture.

BODY ALIGNMENT

You will often see many golfers suffer from poor body alignment, as it is very difficult to diagnose and correct without the aid of video cameras, mirrors or a practice partner.

Good body alignment will increase your ability to deliver the club to the ball at impact, squarely and on target more often, crucial for consistency.

Now you've got the correct stance and posture we need to make sure that we have aligned our knees, hips and shoulders correctly...and we again refer to the Ball to Target Line.

With two batons laid on the ground parallel to each other (you can also use clubs), and having taken your stance and posture, we can then do a very simple check to make sure that you are aiming your body correctly. Make sure that your toes are an equal distance from the baton closest to you.

You should gently flex your knees and ensure that your weight is towards the balls of your feet. Simply place a club across both knees, and check that the club is parallel to the batons on the floor. If your knees are lined up correctly your hips should naturally follow suit.

Shoulder alignment is a little trickier as this is where you are going to need a friend to help you. Take your stance and get in to your now perfect posture position, ready to hit the ball. Next, get a friend to stand to your right and double check that your feet, knees and hips are aligned with the clubs on the floor, and that you are aiming to your target. Get ready to hit the ball and ask your friend to lay a club across the top of your chest and shoulders. This will show whether you are lined up correctly, and that your shoulders are now in line with rest of your body.

TOP TIP:
PAUSE AND RELEASE

IF PAUSING MOMENTARILY AT THE TOP OF YOUR SWING FEELS NATURAL, YOU AREN'T RUSHING YOUR BACKSWING

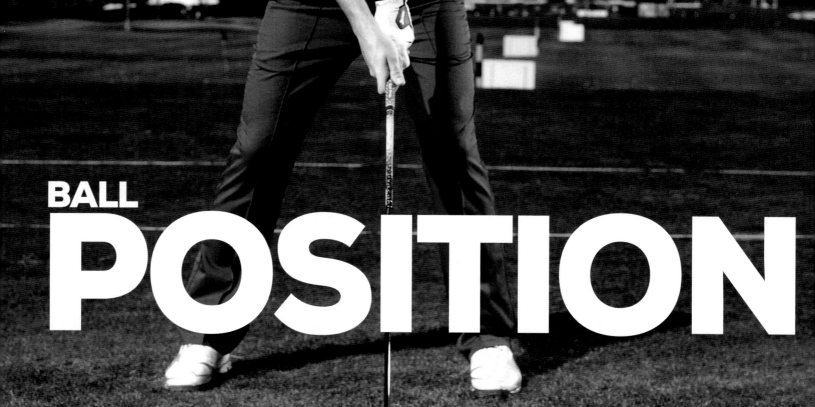

BALL
POSITION

Always check your ball position by laying your clubs down when you practise

WEATHER CONSIDERATIONS

In windy and wet conditions it is always best to have the ball slightly back in the stance to make sure you get a cleaner, lower strike and trajectory

WIND

When playing into the wind don't be afraid to adjust the height of the tee peg lower. If you're downwind tee the ball higher to use the wind to get loft. The lower your ball flies, the less the wind will affect it

BEFORE YOU START

With your driver, make sure that once you've tee'd the ball up and positioned the club behind the ball that the top leading edge of the club is in line with the equator of the ball. With irons, you should tee your ball up about 1 cm off the grass

Where you place the ball in your stance at address is very important, and is sometimes overlooked and under-practised. Many golfers seem to play how they feel most comfortable, with their ball position changing every time they play. With the majority of clubs in your bag, the aim is to strike the ball with a descending blow at the bottom of your down swing – making contact with the ball first and turf second.

If your ball position is too far forward it can result in either hitting the ground first (fatting, as above) or catching the ball halfway up, causing a thinned shot or even topping the ball. However, when playing from the tee with your driver or three wood, the technique changes slightly and the aim is to hit the ball on the upward part of the of the swing, sweeping the ball cleanly off the tee peg.

1 There are many ways to achieve the correct ball position for your shot, but we will look at the two easiest. Before doing this, however, we need to define what we mean when we describe the ball as being at the back or front of the stance.

2 When you take the address position, having placed your feet shoulder width apart, the middle of the stance directly between your legs is actually classed as the back of the stance.

3 For a right-handed golfer, when the ball position is inside the left foot, the ball is classed as at the front of the stance. Reverse this if you are a left-handed golfer.

THE **STATIC** BALL POSITION

This is where the ball position stays the same, regardless of the club you're using. The ball is placed around two inches inside the left foot, and if the club you use gets shorter, simply narrow your stance.

The driver and three wood off the tee peg provide the only exception to this rule, when the ball is always played from inside your left foot. This encourages you to hit the ball on the up swing.

THE **PROGRESSIVE** BALL POSITION

This is both the most natural ball position, and the most commonly used. We feel it brings the best results. Starting with your driver, the ball position moves progressively back in the stance as the clubs get shorter. The ball eventually ends up at the back of the stance, with the short irons and wedges.

HOW TO AIM

While you may adapt certain rules to suit your style when playing golf, one fundamental thing never changes – where you aim. It is the one constant from which a good swing and consistent game will help you gradually improve.

The principle behind aim is called the Ball To Target Line, and applies to every club. Whether you are a professional or a beginner, many shots you hit off line, or bad swings you make, can be traced back to the use of the Ball To Target Line. Let's take a look at how to ensure you're getting it right.

Firstly we lay down a baton (you can also use a club) pointing at the target. This is the Ball to Target Line.

REMEMBER

Always aim at a target 150 yds away - whether you're using a wedge or driver - it's important to have a point of reference. Next, pick a spot (old divot, discoloured grass etc.) a yard in front of you in line with your above target, as when you're at address it is easier to line up with an object that's close, rather than 150 yds away

WIND

Always take into account the wind. For crosswinds it's always a good idea to practise on the range so that you can get an appreciation of how the ball flies in wind. A 10MPH wind can have a 15 yard effect on the ball

STRATEGY

When out of position always aim for the heart of the green, so as not to compound an error

3 Grip the club. We must now get the clubface positioned squarely to your Ball to Target Line.

2 We then place a second club on the ground parallel to the first one. We call this your Body to Target Line.

4 You aim the club simply by placing the leading edge of the club at right angles to the Ball to Target Line, resting the sole of the club on the ground behind the ball.

BUILD A GREAT
SWING

ADDRESS POSITION

There are literally hundreds of different theories on how the golf club should be swung, but if you strip away all the technical jargon and get down to the meat and bones of the tuition, everyone is actually teaching very similar principles.

To make things simple we are not going to diagnose swing faults, as there are literally hundreds of reasons why your swing might not be working, so if you are having serious problems we'd recommend seeking help from your local PGA professional.

Here, we are going to concentrate on the six main swing sections, explaining how they work and how each swing path will affect the way the ball flies.

KEY DO AND DON'T

Don't rush it. Snatching the club back at the start of the swing is a classic mistake. Do practise with all the clubs in your bag, and practising on your weaknesses will benefit your game in the long run. Balance is key because if your balance is off it will cause you to sway, making striking the golf ball harder

REMEMBER

The swing starts with a shoulder turn, and not a hand movement. Make sure your hands are in line with the ball at the address – never behind it

SWING THOUGHT

A rhythmical swing is a good one

Address Position 1
This is also known as the Set Up Position, and is the position you will take as you prepare to make the first movements of the golf swing.

This is also where you start to build your Pre-Shot 2
Routine. You should go through the grip, aim, stance, posture, body alignment and finally ball position routines, keeping in mind any variants to adopt depending on which club you're using.

YOUR BACKSWING

This is the first major part of the golf swing, and is also known as the Takeaway.

1 Depending on what club you're using, 60% of your weight should favour the right side of your body. Make sure that your hands are in line with the ball.

2 Start to turn your shoulders and hips, keeping your head still and eyes on the ball.

5

3

4

Keep your left arm as straight as possible, but start to rotate the hands and forearms so that the clubface remains square to the swing path.

Keep rotating your shoulders and hips until your left shoulder is under your chin. You should find your right knee is still flexed, and that as you've turned your weight has shifted further to the right side of your body, like a tightening spring.

SWING PLANE

This is the angle at which you swing the club round your body (see page 33 for a description of each swing path). Getting the swing plane wrong can cause many faults in your golf swing, negatively affecting your ability to deliver the club to the ball on the correct path.

A swing plane that is too upright will make the angle of attack too steep, meaning you will tend to cause an out-to-in swing path. If the angle of attack is too shallow and the swing plane is too flat, you will hit at the ball with an inside-to-out swing path.

Your swing plane will change for every club, quite simply because as the clubs get longer, the taller you stand when addressing the ball.

WEATHER CONSIDERATIONS

Playing in waterproofs will make your swing more restricted, so make sure you completely turn your shoulder – it is crucial that you fully execute the backswing

WIND

Into the wind don't be afraid to take a couple of extra clubs, but remember to swing smoothly - being aggressive will cause the ball to balloon high into the air

BEFORE YOU START

Always double check your alignment before going to hit the ball

CHANGE OF DIRECTION

This is the point where your backswing stops and your downswing starts. Once you have completed the backswing, pause at the top and then drop your hands slightly towards the ground. As you do so, start to move your weight back towards your left side...like a spring starting to recoil after being compressed.

DOWNSWING

The club continues down while your hips and shoulders turn, ensuring the club starts its path towards the ground slightly inside the backswing path and inside the Ball to Target Line.

EXECUTION

This is the part of the swing where your body is uncoiling, with your weight (driving towards the ball) accelerating the club head through the hitting area.

At this point we also need to talk about the three swing paths.

SWING PATHS

INSIDE-TO-OUT

This is where the club attacks the ball from inside your Ball to Target Line, and continues on a path out of it. If your clubface is aiming at the flag when it impacts the ball you will find that the ball initially starts towards the flag, but ultimately hooks left.

OUTSIDE-TO-IN

This is where the club attacks the ball from outside of the Ball to Target Line and continues on a path inside of it. If the clubface is again pointing at the flag when it impacts you will find the ball starts towards the target but finally curves right of the target.

SQUARE-INSIDE-SQUARE

This is the perfect swing path, and will ensure that as long as the clubface is aiming at the target through impact you will hit straight golf shots every time.

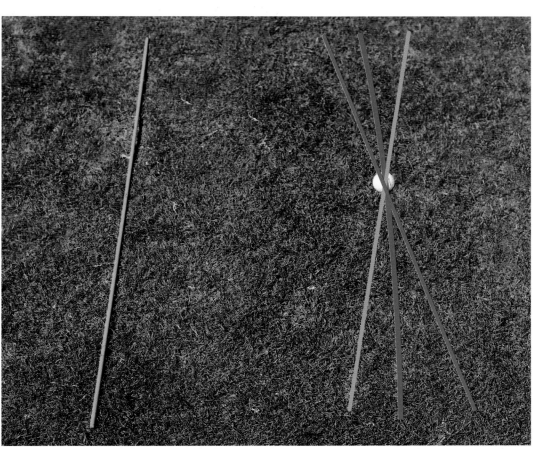

PGA LESSON

A lot of things happen very quickly through the execution of the golf swing, and it's almost impossible to see the intricacies of what's going on with the naked eye. This is why, when you have a lesson with your PGA pro, they will usually have a video camera with which to record you, allowing them to play your swing back in slow motion.

When your swing is slowed down you will be able to see that the forearms and hands rotate and release through the hit, that your hips and shoulders start to turn through the shot, and that your weight will start to transfer to the left side of your body.

FOLLOW THROUGH

This is also light-heartedly known as posing for the camera, but is an important part of the swing. As you can see from the picture, right, the swing is complete and your weight is now balanced on the left side of your body. Also note that the hips, torso, shoulders and head are pointing towards the target and that the club is now resting behind the neck. This position is essential, as not completing the follow through can cause many faults, from deceleration of club head speed to the dreaded shanks, when you strike the ball with the heel of your club.

You should always commit yourself to the golf shot, and always accelerate the club through the ball no matter which club you are using or shot you are trying to play.

THE SWING
IN MOTION

We have put together a complete flow of the golf swing, side on, to give you an overall picture of what the swing should look like.

MASTER YOUR
WOODS

Now we've covered the key fundamentals, we can move onto explaining how to go about mastering some of the key shots you'll use every time you step on to the golf course.

The first thing that we do on the golf course is tee off, so let's look at the techniques used to hit the ball off the tee with the driver and three wood.

The unique thing about teeing off is that it's the only time you are allowed to use a tee peg. Notice the ball is at three different heights for the three different clubs below.

As you can see with the irons, the ball is fractionally above grass level and this is because we need to hit the ball with a descending blow.

The three woods and utility clubs need the ball sitting around a centimeter above the grass, promoting you to hit the ball slightly on the upswing. You will also need to alter your ball position for these clubs, moving it closer to your left instep.

With the driver and three wood you will notice you are standing much further away from the ball, and that the ball position has moved forward in the stance (opposite the inside of the left heel). The ball should be teed up so that top edge of the club is lined up with the middle of the ball.

We are now going to start the swing. Hovering the club behind the ball with your weight 60-40 in favour of the right side, rotate your shoulders back to the top of your swing, making sure that your shoulders have turned 90 degrees and that your back is now pointing towards the target.

KEY DO AND DON'T

With the driver and 3-wood off the tee, make sure the ball is an inch inside your left heel at address. Don't have the ball too far forward – it'll throw your alignment out and cause you to over extend your swing. Ball too far back in the stance will mean you're hitting down too much, and will not enable you to sweep the ball cleanly off the tee peg

REMEMBER

A driver isn't always the best policy, 3-woods and long irons will give you more accuracy in all situations, so consider that if distance isn't an issue. Playing for position is always beneficial

SWING THOUGHT

A smooth, sweeping action is required. Try to hit the ball cleanly, as opposed to hitting down on the ball and hitting divots (as you would with irons)

HOW IMPORTANT

It's important to practise your woods, but don't be tempted to do so at the expense of your short game

WEATHER CONSIDERATIONS

Into the wind and crosswind tee the ball down lower. Downwind, tee it high and let it fly

After a slight pause start the downswing, keeping it as wide as possible, accelerating the club and turning your whole body through the hitting area. Your left arm should remain straight through this part of the swing, to make sure you deliver the club head to the ball correctly.

Continue the club up and around to the top of the swing and hold the finish position, balanced and composed.

A smooth, balanced swing is what's needed to hit the driver and three woods successfully, too often you'll see people trying to smash the ball miles, and only reach the 100 yard flag.

TOP TIP:

TIGER TEMPAH

PROTECTING YOUR DRIVER WITH A HEADCOVER IS IMPORTANT, THEY ARE SURPRISINGLY FRAGILE THINGS THAT NEED LOOKING AFTER

MASTER YOUR UTILITY AND
LONG IRONS

Long irons (3, 4, and 5) are typically the hardest clubs in the bag to use, so over the last 10 years golf companies have started to make Utility, Hybrid or Rescue clubs – which are easier to hit – as a replacement. These clubs are designed with the same technology used in drivers and three woods and, as mentioned above, are much easier to use.

SETUP

Place the club head behind the ball aiming at the target, settle in the shot remembering to place the feet shoulder width apart parallel to the Ball To Target line.

At this point the ball position should be slightly forward in the stance, closer to the inside of the left foot. Make sure that your hands are now in line with the ball and that your weight is evenly distributed.

TECHNIQUE

With the club behind ball, start to turn the shoulders and hips, keeping the left arm straight for as long as you can. At the top of the back swing make sure that your left shoulder is under your chin, that your back is pointing to the target and that your hips have turned 45 degrees. Your weight should now be over your right leg and you should feel tension in the right knee.

Next, start to turn the shoulders and hips towards the target, driving the club on the correct swing plane. With the left arm now completely straight, release the hands through the hit zone, striking the ball crisply. Your weight will now be over the left side of your body and your hips and shoulders will have turned nearly 45 degrees through the shot.

Continue to the top of the swing so that your shoulders, chest and hips are now pointing at the target and your weight is completely over the left leg.

Continue the club up to the top of the swing balanced and in control.

KEY DO AND DON'T

Always practise with your long irons and utility woods, as mastering these will significantly benefit your mid iron shots too. This is the weakest part in most golfers' game, but that's because it's the hardest. Utility clubs should be used more like a long iron, so make sure you hit ball then turf (hitting down on the back of the ball). This creates more spin on the ball, helping it get airborne for you

REMEMBER

Utilities can be used for chip and runs around the fringe of the green, they help to get the ball in the air

SWING THOUGHT

Make sure you commit to the shot, hitting through to the target. Not committing properly can cause an inconsistent strike, open or close the club, and in general cause problems with distance and accuracy

TOP TIP

Commitment is key – but don't rush the swing. Make sure you complete the backswing – if the swing's too short it will become rushed and out of synch with the rest of your body. Also, long irons out of the rough are notoriously difficult to control. A safer bet is to use a more lofted club (loft always helps in the rough) in getting to safety

Remember to be balanced and in control at all times.

MASTER YOUR MID &
SHORT IRONS

GET TO KNOW YOUR CLUBS

The middle irons (6, 7, 8) and the short irons (9, PW, SW, LW) are also known as the scoring clubs, and play a vital part in successful golf. The key to good iron play is controlling how far the ball travels, and this is only possible when you're hitting with consistency. Here are a few key points to consider when playing iron shots, and some vital information for successful execution in this area of the game.

1. Understand the club and how it works
2. Set up for success, follow earlier procedures
3. The club does the up. Resist the lift
4. Distance control, so know your yardages

1 The irons are all bent forwards, which gives us a clue as to their function. The shaft comes out the head of the club, and leans towards the target. This suggests the club is designed to be hit on the downswing, hitting the ball before the ground.

2 The amount the shaft leans forward determines where the ball is hit in the swing arc. All iron shots require you to set up with your hands in front of the clubhead and ball. With the wedges, the shaft will lean further forward, and to compensate this we need to place the ball nearer the middle of the stance. As the club length increases, shaft lean decreases, meaning we should move the ball towards the target. This should produce a straight line from the left shoulder through the hands and down to the clubhead, which is angled forward.

3 The ball leaves the ground thanks to a combination of club loft and backspin. Without the latter the ball will simply not leave the ground. Many common errors associated with hitting mid and short-irons occur when the club overtakes your hands in an attempt to give the ball lift. This leads to unreliable striking and inconsistent loft at impact, both of which make distance control very hard. All other sports use one bat/racket and it is the player's responsibility to lift the ball; with golf you have 14 different lofted clubs, which means you don't have to generate lift as the club does this for you. A simple way of thinking about this is that we control the forward movement of the ball, while the club controls the height.

4 Once a consistent strike is achieved You can then start to get an idea of how far each club travels. The

important thing to realise is that there is such a range of clubs available to you you'll rarely need to swing a club at full tilt – a common error. It is important to understand that the golf swing needs to be smooth in its transition from backswing to downswing, and this ensures the club stays on plane (and most importantly that your hands stay ahead of the clubhead). You will find more accuracy from developing two yardages with each club at first, one with a full swing and one with a ¾ swing. This will allow you to choose the appropriate shot for each situation you find yourself in.

KEY DO AND DON'T

Do practise these as much as possible, as they are your scoring irons. Play within yourself, don't be a hero. Know your yardages with every club, particularly how far the ball carries to maximise your scoring opportunities and avoid hazards. Don't try to guide the ball onto the target – pick a spot and hit at it

REMEMBER

You're looking to hit the ball with a descending blow to create as much backspin and carry as possible

SWING THOUGHT

A full shoulder turn and commit to hitting down and through to your target

BEFORE YOU START

When you practise or warm up, start with the short irons, as their diminutive size give your limbs the biggest stretch

STRATEGY

Always leave your favourite distance into the green to maximise the scoring opportunity. Full shots are easier to control than half shots

THE SHORT GAME

Around 70% of golf is played within 70 yards of the flag, and it is why we feel the short game is one of the most important parts of golfing. Ironically, it's probably also one of the most overlooked and under practised. This is one part of the game that will make or break your round of golf, and it's where the professionals tend to spend – along with putting – at least 60% of their practice time.

Most top professionals will miss at least four or five greens in a round of golf, but the one thing they have in their arsenal is the ability to scramble the ball up and down on a regular basis.

The stats don't lie: on the PGA Tour during 2012 only 40% of putts were holed from 10 feet, compared to 96% of putts holed from five feet or less. This shows how important getting the ball as close to the hole as possible from 70 yards and under is and practising this part of the game with good technique will reduce your scores and handicaps hugely.

We are going to go through the three short game disciplines of pitching, chipping and bunker play, and show you the different techniques used to get the ball close to the flag.

PITCHING

This shot is played from a maximum of 70 yards away from the green and is, quite simply, a shortened version of the full swing. Club selection is always dictated by what you have in front of you. If there is a bunker or water hazard to negotiate then you will need to take a more lofted club (gaining you height) to take the trouble out of play. If there is nothing between you and the hole then you can take a less lofted club and run the ball in to the flag.

If the flag is tucked away behind a bunker or hazard, think about playing it safe as playing a bad pitch shot will only compound the mistake, and cause you to drop more shots.

There are only a couple of subtle changes to the regular swing that we need to make.

Grip down on the selected club by an inch. This will give you a little more control and feel.

KEY DO AND DON'T

Don't rush the shot. Do take your time and get it right, as these are the shots that will win you points

REMEMBER

Pitch from no further than 70 yds. Always err on the side of caution and don't be afraid to play away from the flag or danger – percentage shots are always more rewarding

WEATHER CONSIDERATION

If it's wet the ball tends to skid more, so use a more lofted club and make the ball land softer. If the greens are soft pitch the ball directly at the hole (it'll stop more quickly)

WIND

Wind won't effect the direction too much, but will affect distance control. Into the wind take more club and swing smoother. Downwind take more loft, so that the ball lands softly

HOW IMPORTANT

20% of your short game practice should be pitching

TOP TIP

Know your personal yardages with your shorter irons for different shots, it makes club selection and tactics a lot easier

Narrow your stance slightly. This will force the swing slightly upright and help you hit down onto the back of the ball, creating more spin.

Also open your stance slightly, so your feet aim just left of your target.

With aiming you need to imagine how the ball will fly, and this will only come with practice. Spending time learning how each club (and the ball) behaves will greatly reduce the amount of shots you take in a round, and will have the biggest effect in reducing your handicap.

Remember to always accelerate the club through the hit and complete your follow through.

THE NEW MP-S TOUR BALL

The ball that loves to spin.

CHIPPING

Chipping around the greens is simple as long as we adopt the correct principles, which are different to pitching. We are going to work on the ten yard chip shot, and once we have this technique it is easily adapted to longer chip shots, simply by playing around with both the length of swing and club type. Chip shots can not only be played with the sand iron, but also regular irons, utility clubs and even fairway woods.

We first have to take a few things into consideration before determining which club to use:

1. How is the ball lying

2. How close are we to the putting surface

3. How far onto the green is the flag

We are going to assume that the ball is lying on the fringe of the green and that the flag is 15 paces from the edge of the green.

For this kind of shot we would recommend using a pitching wedge or 9-iron.

SET UP

Notice above how the feet are closer together, and that we have taken hold of the club at the bottom of the grip. We have moved the ball so that it is inside the right foot and have shifted our weight onto our left side.

Because we have gripped right down on the club you will notice that we are standing much closer to the ball.

TECHNIQUE

Keeping your left arm straight and hands ahead of the ball, start to turn the shoulders and take the club away to the seven o'clock position, maintaining the angles shown below in the wrist and arms.

Then, simply accelerate the club down on to the back of the ball, again maintaining the angles and keeping the hands ahead of the ball, holding the finish at 4 o'clock.

What you are trying to do with the chip shot is get the ball to land directly on the green, as chipping the ball into the fringe or rough first can cause the ball to bounce off line.

You will also need to take in to account the slopes on the green and how the ball breaks (see page 65).

Below we have put together a simple diagram, which shows how different clubs perform when playing the chip shot.

CHIPPING

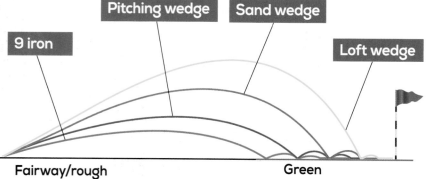

9 iron
Pitching wedge
Sand wedge
Loft wedge

Fairway/rough
Green

KEY DO AND DON'T

Always look to land the ball onto the putting surface first. Always allow for break - read the greens as you would a putt. Try and get the ball within a dustbin lid of the hole. Don't try anything too Hollywood, it is unlikely to come off. A bad putt is always better than a bad chip - if you're close enough to putt, do so

SWING THOUGHT

Always hit down onto the back of the ball to make sure of a clean strike

HOW IMPORTANT

40% of your short game practise should be spent chipping. It's that important

WEATHER CONDITIONS

In some conditions a club such as a 5-wood might be required to chip out of mud

BEFORE YOU START

A ball in long rough will need aggression to get out, but be careful because lack of spin will mean it won't stop as quick. Before your round at a new course, hit a couple of balls onto the edge of a putting green to get a feel for how they run

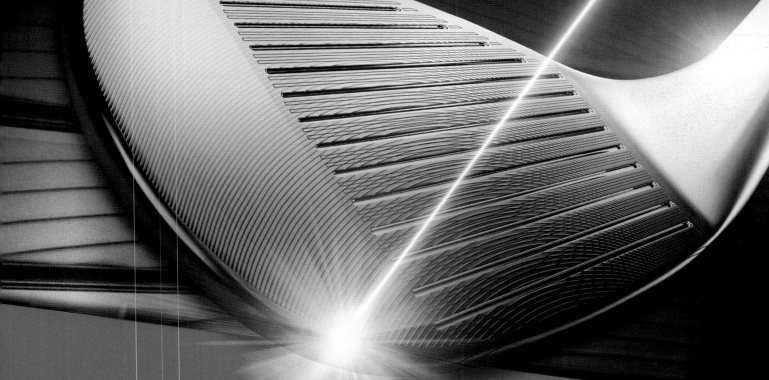

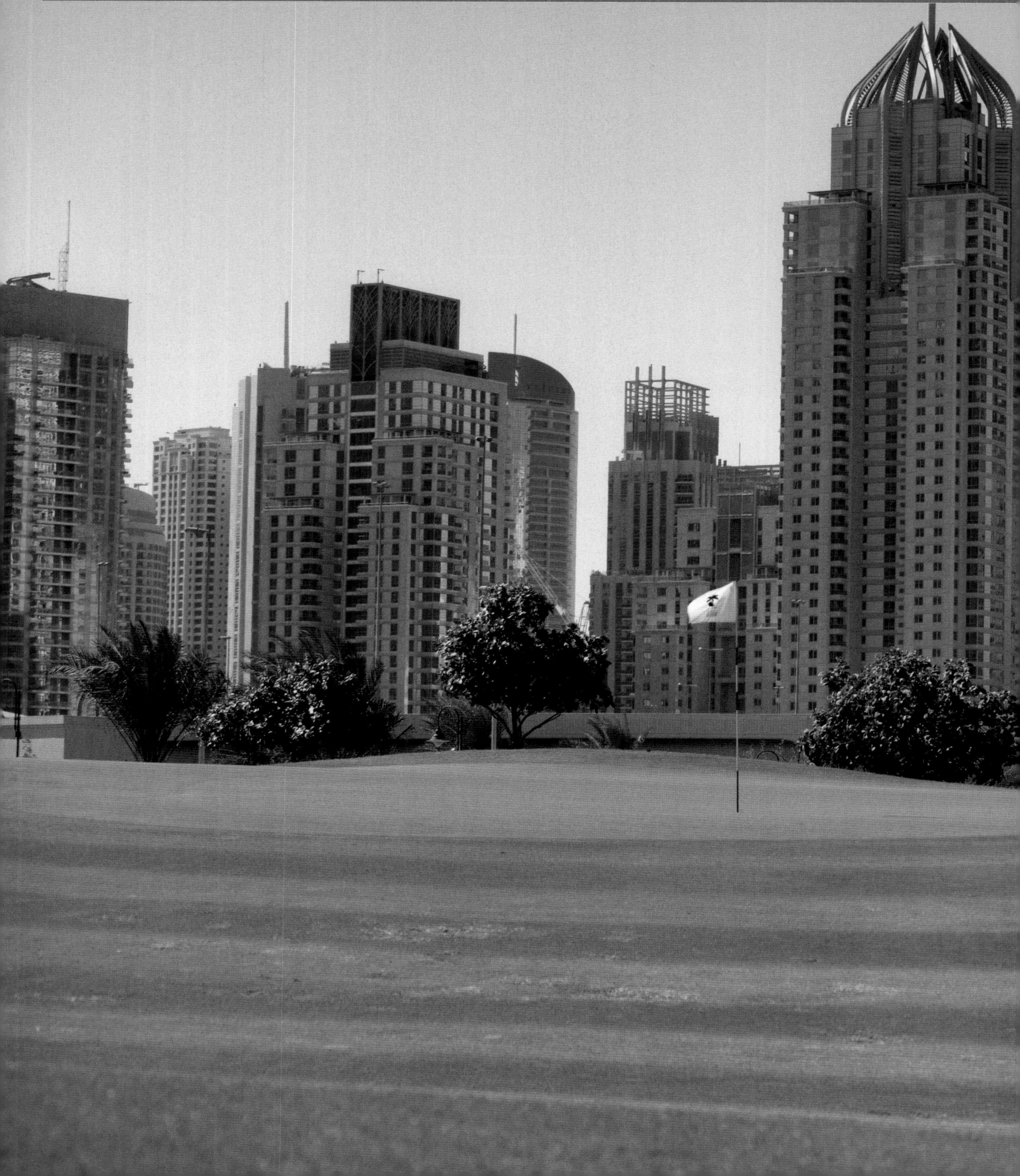

TOP TIP: PRE-ROUND PRACTICE

BEFORE A ROUND AT A NEW COURSE, PRACTICE A FEW CHIPS ONTO THE GREEN TO GET A FEEL FOR HOW THEY RUN

THE BUNKER SHOT

This shot probably causes more sleepless nights than any other, but it's actually surprisingly easy to play. It is the only shot in the game where you are looking to actively miss the ball, and once we understand why the sand iron is designed as it is, and how it performs, we'll have you flying out of those bunkers with relative ease.

▲
AIM
The rules change slightly with this shot, as you don't aim directly at the flag. Start by taking and open stance, which means that your feet, knees, hips and shoulders should pointing left of the target.

Don't panic about the ball coming out to the left as you are going to be opening the clubface to compensate for this.

▲
BALL POSITION
You move the ball forward in the stance, closer to where you play the long irons and three woods from.

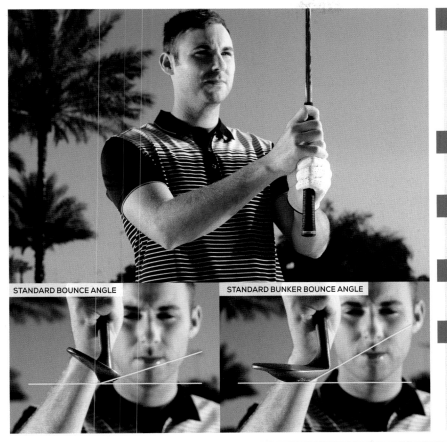

STANDARD BOUNCE ANGLE

STANDARD BUNKER BOUNCE ANGLE

KEY DO AND DON'T

Always accelerate the club through the hit, but no more than usual. In the spirit of course etiquette, always rake the bunker after you've finished in it. Touching the sand with your club before you've played you're shot will see you incur a penalty stroke – don't do it

REMEMBER

The ball comes out on a cushion of sand, so always try to hit the sand at least an inch behind the ball

HOW IMPORTANT

As with chipping, 40% of your short game practice should be spent in the sand

WEATHER CONDITIONS

The ball comes out a lot faster from wet sand, and as a result goes a lot further. Take it slightly easier

BEFORE YOU START

Always enter the bunker from behind. If you fail to hit your ball out first time, you don't want it rolling back into your footprint. Remember, you can't always do full practice swings as you're not allowed to touch the sand

▲ THE CLUB

First of all, take a normal hold, but do this half way down the grip, as shown above. Then turn the club in your hands so that the clubface is at a 45 degree angle, this is called opening the clubface, and it not only improves the loft on the club, but also increases its bounce, meaning it won't dig into sand.

▲ GETTING READY TO HIT

Remember that if you ground your club in the sand at anytime while your ball remains in the bunker, you incur a shot penalty. This is why you see the pros hover the club in the sand before hitting.

TECHNIQUE

You have to create a stable base in the sand, and to do this wiggle your feet until you feel your stance is secure. This also gives you an idea of the texture and depth of the sand.

You are now ready to start making the swing, and what you need to do is focus on where you are physically going to make contact with the ball. Unlike the other shots in golf where you are focusing on the back of the ball, here you are looking for the club to enter the sand at least one inch behind the ball. Hitting the sand here causes an explosion and the ball actually comes out of the bunker on a cushion of sand (see below right).

The swing path should be along the line of your feet, making it feel as if you are cutting across and underneath the ball.

For the longer bunker shots it is always best to use the same technique as above, but with a different club. By using a pitching wedge the force of the explosion is accented forward rather than up, leaving the ball to run lower and further.

▲ When you are practising it is always a good idea to draw a line in the sand an inch behind the ball and focus on hitting the line every time.

▲ The swing is slightly abbreviated and is what we call a three quarter swing. But the key to this shot is that we are always accelerating the club through the sand and that the follow through is the same length as the back swing.

▲ The only way you can hope to master this shot is by plenty of practice. By doing so you will be able to hit the ball different lengths and varying heights.

DESIGNED FOR THE TOUR GUYS
BY THE TOUR GUYS

THE NEW
MP
LINE FROM
MIZUNO

Mizuno has been committed to understanding the needs of professional golfers since we first introduced our golf equipment from Japan in the 1970's.

The quality and consistency of manufacture immediately set us apart from the crowd, and subsequently made such an impression that in 1986 the European Tour asked us to run our first official equipment workshop. Twenty-seven years later, Mizuno is still the official workshop to the European Tour and The Open Championship.

With such an extensive and illustrious history on tour, we understand what better players like in their equipment. As a result, our tour players can use Mizuno's standard production heads (still forged at the same exclusive factory in Hiroshima, Japan) straight out of the box.

Every year on tour teaches us something new, but our philosophy of producing exceptional quality remains the same. That's what makes our MP Series so special.

#nothingfeelslikeamizuno

TOP TIP: LINE IN THE SAND

WHEN PRACTISING BUNKER SHOTS, DRAW A LINE IN THE SAND AN INCH BEHIND YOUR BALL AND PRACTISE CONSISTANTLY HITTING THAT LINE

THE ART OF
PUTTING

Putting is a game within a game: over 40% of golf is played on the putting surface. It seems such a simple part of the game, but a few putts missed here and there can ruin a round of golf and affect your handicap.

THE NEW **VERSA**
BY ODYSSEY

VISIONARY HIGH CONTRAST ALIGNMENT

ONE DEGREE OFF IS ONE DEGREE OUT.

THE VERSA #1

IMPROVE YOUR
ALIGNMENT AND
LOWER YOUR SCORES.
ODYSSEYGOLF.COM/VERSA

#1 PUTTER IN GOLF.®

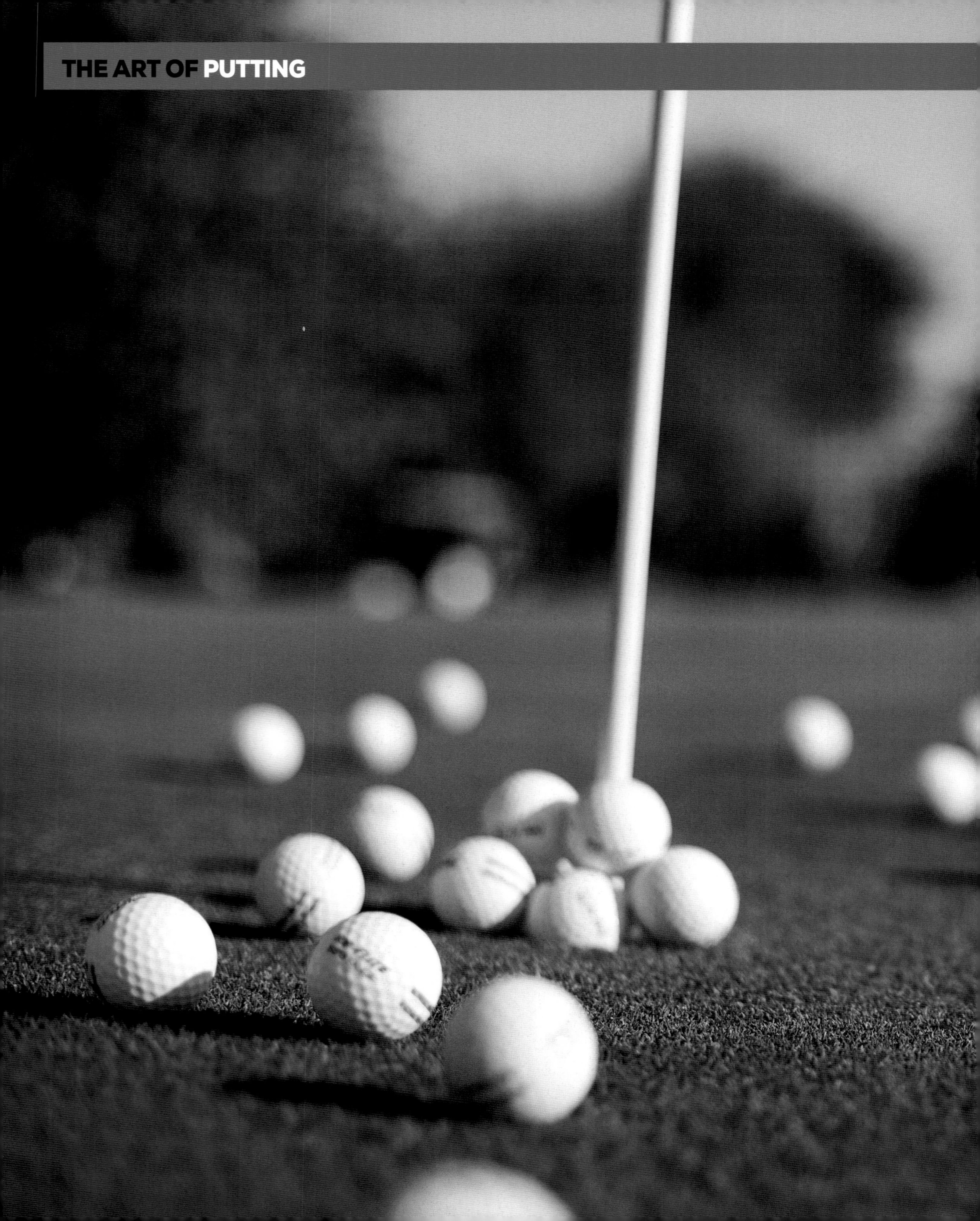

TOP TIP:

GREEN MACHINE

THE STATS POINT TO THE GREEN AS BEING THE PLACE A ROUND OF GOLF CAN BE MADE OR BROKEN, SO GET ON THE PRACTISE GREENS

Many golfers don't spend enough time on their putting technique, settling for a few putts on the practice green before heading onto the course, yet they expect to hole putts with ease. When practising your short game you should spend at least 40% of time putting, and at least 15 minutes on the practise green before you play. The best players in the world spend hours every week at each tournament making sure they are used to the pace and slopes of the greens, and that their technique is finely tuned.

We have broken our tuition down into two sections, Technique and Holing Out.

First up Rob Leonard, Head PGA professional from Harpendon Common Golf Club, is going to take you through the technique, setup and reading the of the greens.

Next, we are extremely privileged to have Ian Poulter, Ryder Cup hero and multiple tournament winner, to help us with holing out. Ian is probably the best putter in the world, and on page 66 he gives us a fascinating insight into how he approaches his putts, and the practice drills he does.

TECHNIQUE

HOLD/GRIP

There are a few different grips used these days, but they all have one thing in common: they aim to reduce the amount the wrists hinge during your stroke, in a bid for increased control and consistency.

You will notice that a putter's physical grip is radically different from all the other clubs in that it features a flat surface. There are many different styles, shapes and sizes of putter grip available, and we would suggest that – with the help of a PGA professional – you try as many as possible. It's very easy to change a putter's grip, and you must select one that not only feels comfortable, but also helps with your putting strokes.

We are going to take you through how to apply the two styles of grip used by the best players in the world.

REVERSE OVERLAP ▶

This grip has been sported by 85% of major winners over the last 40 years, and is used by the likes of Tiger Woods and Rory McIlroy.

Place your left hand on the putter grip, with the side of the grip running along the lifeline, next gently wrap your fingers around the grip, resting your thumb along its flat front side.

Raise the forefinger of your left hand, then apply your right hand in the same way as we've just done with the left, making sure the right side of the grip runs along the lifelines. Gently wrap your fingers around the grip, again placing the thumb down the flat centre. To complete the grip, just rest the forefinger of your left hand over the little finger of the right. This will help lock the hands together, helping them work as a unit. The palms should now be facing each other, with the back of your left hand pointing towards the target.

◄ LEFT HAND BELOW RIGHT

There are many golfers that use this grip, as they feel it keeps their wrists stiffer and more stable through the stroke. It also helps them balance their shoulder out.

The process is exactly the same as the reverse overlap (left), but here the hands are swapped around.

Ultimately both grips will give you a stable hold, but it's up to you to find out which suits your game best.

KEY DO AND DON'T

However far back you take the putter, accelerate through the same distance the other side. Don't move your head until after you've hit the ball, doing so will effect where the ball goes

REMEMBER

Grip pressure is light, more of a hold. Not like an irons grip. Also remember the ball will always take the majority of break (turn) as it starts to lose speed

SWING THOUGHT

Rhythm, smooth back then accelerate the putter through the ball

HOW IMPORTANT

40% of all short game practise should be spent putting

WEATHER CONSIDERATIONS

The green will be a lot slower in the wet, so be more aggressive and direct with your putting

WIND

As always, widen your stance in the wind to create a more stable base

BEFORE YOU START

Always spend 15 minutes on a putting surface getting used to the pace and break (curl or turn) of the greens

STRATEGY

Aim to get enough power on the ball to get it 18 inches past the hole. 99% of putts left short don't go in, so be bold

◄ STANCE AND POSTURE

As with all shots, good putting requires a comfortable, sturdy base to work from, and to do this we place the feet shoulder width apart. While holding the putter you should bend from the hips until your eyes are over the ball, and settle into the posture by gently flexing your knees until you feel comfortable and balanced.

You will find that we have created a 'V' angle, this shape must be maintained throughout the stroke to make sure that the putter is delivered to the ball consistently.

BALL POSITION AND STROKE

We place the ball just forward of centre in the stance, this because we are trying to strike it slightly on the up swing to promote topspin, which also reduces the amount the ball skids before rolling.

The stroke itself is very simple; we just need to follow three simple steps:

1 Keep your head still, locking your wrists and elbows. Your head is the centre point of the axis, and the putter head is the weight, just like the pendulum of a grandfather clock.

2 Simply rock the shoulders back and through. A nice smooth back swing is required, and always remember to accelerate the putter through the ball. You will find that the putter path will be inside on the way back, square through the hit and inside on the follow through.

3 Keep your eyes down. Its always tempting to try and look up as soon you make contact with the ball, but this causes the shoulders to move out of line and will affect not only the strike, but also the direction of the ball.

▲ ALIGNMENT

Once you have established how the ball is going to turn or break, (which we look at on the opposite page) pick a point to aim at. This will not only be a target line, but also your eye line and line of sight. Place the putter squarely on this line and then move your feet so that your stance is parallel to the target line.

PRACTICE DRILLS

1 Feel

Put down five tee pegs at five feet intervals, and putt to each tee in turn. Spend at least the first 10 minutes of you practise doing this and you will find you quickly get a decent feel for the pace of the greens.

2 Stroke - Chalk Line

This is a great drill to ensure your putting is both on line and consistent. Simply find a straight 10-foot and use a chalk liner (available at all good DIY shops) and mark the putt. This will give a line on the green which acts as your target and eye line. Place you feet parallel to this line and start hitting putts. Do this for at least ten minutes and you will find you are soon holing the putt with relative ease.

3 Breaks

Simply putting around the practise green to all the holes in turn will give you all the breaks practise you need. Having said that, spending a few minutes just hitting left to right and right to left putts will give you extra confidence when you are out on the course.

READING GREENS

As Ian Poulter details over the page, the more you practise putting, the better you will become at reading a green. You will very rarely play on a flat green, and understanding that the ball will always role to the lowest part of the green is crucial. There are a couple of key factors that need to be taken into account when looking for the perfect putting line.

1 How hard am I going to have to hit the putt? You are looking to hit the ball with perfect pace, and the power should be such that if the putt is missed your ball will only run 18 inches past the hole. Also consider that the harder you have to hit the putt the less the ball will turn, and that downhill putts always turn more than uphill putts.

2 If you ever play golf abroad, you might come across a green that has what's called grain. This is when the grasses are grown coarse and strong, which effects how the ball rolls. Down grain putts will be faster than if you putt into the grain, and the ball also turns more with the grain. You will notice on TV that greens have dark and shiny patches, these show which way the grain runs. Dark patches are where the grain is growing towards you, and shiny patches are when the grain is running away from you.

You should try to break a putt down into three sections when it comes to judging a putt's break. The first third of the putt will tend to run straight, because of the ball skidding. The second third takes over as the ball starts to roll and take the break. The third section happens as the ball starts to loose its pace and roll out, here the ball will turn the most.

You should try to build up a picture in your mind's eye of how the ball will turn and you should always walk around the putt before hitting it. Walking the full 360 degrees around the putt will give you a better picture of all the slopes, giving you more of a feel for how hard the putt should to be hit.

HOLING OUT WITH
IAN POULTER

As an avid golfer, you'll have come across numerous people keen to offer their two pence worth on the dark art of sinking a putt. However, from my time on the Tour I've learned the only things you really need are a clear head and a healthy chunk of aggression – the rest is just practise. Let's take a look at how to go about it.

WELCOME

Before we kick on with the tuition, let's take a quick look at how my tour colleagues and I go about setting up a putt, and the thinking that goes behind the routine.

When it's my turn to putt, I place the ball down on the green in front of my coin with just the dimples showing. As you can see the Titleist logo and line I tend to add are out of view (image below). This allows me to focus exclusively on the lines of the putter and the line to the target.

You will notice that many pros place the ball down, read the green, adjust the line on their ball if they use one, stand back, check the alignment again and then go back for one final fiddle with the ball. What they are doing is predetermining the line between ball and hole, and as we all know as players, often as you stand over a putt your mindset and perception changes. You think: "actually, I know I've read it left centre but it feels left edge now", so the line on the ball (image below right) is left of centre but now I'm thinking it should be left edge. So do I now stand back again and change the little line on the ball to left edge, or just go ahead and hit the putt? All this faffing overloads the brain, meaning you eventually take too long to hit the putt and make a poor stroke. Trust me when I say a clear head will give better results.

REMEMBER

If you use a line on your ball sometimes your routine is going to take a lot longer

SWING THOUGHT

If you have read the putt correctly, and yet not hit the putt with enough pace, you haven't committed properly to the putt and the line you have just spent time checking will be completely wrong

HOLING OUT AN 8-FOOT PUTT

1 Place the ball in front of your coin with just the dimples showing.

2 Then start your 360 degree look at the putt. I walk to the left side of the putt at 90 degrees, to ascertain whether the putt is up or down hill, and judge if there is any grain to worry about.

3 At this point I have already seen that the putt is up hill and will break from left. The grain is slightly into me, which will make the putt a little slower.

4 I will now move round again directly behind the hole at 180 degrees and crouch down to judge the entire line from ball to hole. I now imagine a painted line from my ball to the hole that carries through two and half feet past the hole. I have stats from the Tour that show from three feet I have holed 100% of putts, this lets me be slightly more aggressive in determining how hard to hit the ball.

5 I then have a quick look from the 270 degree position, just to confirm everything is correct.

6 After that it's a case of getting back behind the ball for one last look. I now have all the information I need, and a 360 degree picture of the putt in my head. All of this has taken no more than 20 seconds.

7 I then walk into my putt and settle into my stance, focusing on the line I have to hit and at what pace. At this stage my posture is slightly back from the ball. I have two practise stokes to confirm the feel and pace I need to get the ball two and half feet past the hole.

8 Finally I move in to the ball and have two quick looks at the hole to make sure I've got my putter and body aimed along the imaginary painted line. I still have the hole in my peripheral vision, and now it's simply a case of pulling the putter back and hitting the putt. Easy.

You – like me – will find that being confident and aggressive with your putting, and not being afraid to hit two feet beyond the pin, will see you hole out more often. Problems come from being too negative and tentative with the putts, 99% of putts left short of the hole will not go in, so go for it.

When hitting the putt I look for the ball to hit the back of the hole just above the cup line, and from six feet very rarely will you see my ball simply drop into the hole – you will see it hit the mud at the back of the hole and drop. However, from inside two feet my putt will hit the cup liner – its just something I have become used to over the last few years.

PRACTICE DRILLS

There's a few practice drills I like to do, and I recommend giving them a go if you're keen to improve your putting game – they've certainly played their part in improving mine.

▼ MARKED BALL

I take a ball and, with a marker pen, draw a line around the circumference. Then I simply find a straight six-foot putt on the green, line up the marked ball with the hole, and hit putts. If the stroke and strike are correct, the line on the ball rolls smoothly along, but if you felt the putter face open or close, the line becomes a blur.

▲ AROUND THE CLOCK

This is a great one for ascertaining how the greens run at a golf course. Set up eight tee pegs around the hole, each six feet out. This will give the putt from 360 degrees, which is exactly what I do when checking the lines of my putts on the course. Start at ball number one, and only finish when you've holed all the putts from one to eight in succession. If you miss number seven, start the process again. I do this at every tournament to get a feel for how the ball rolls and how much the grain affects the turn of the ball. If I have time I will start the pegs three feet from the hole, then move out six feet and then finally nine feet, as this gives me a feel for the greens for the whole week.

RYDER CUP
GLORY

"Being ruthless with my putter during the 2012 Ryder Cup helped me win the final match on Saturday afternoon which, ultimately, proved to be a tipping point for a great European comeback"

PUTTING AIDS

There are two putting aids that I use, but they only really make and appearance once or twice a year for an hour to check everything is working properly.

The first gadget I use is called the PathFinder, and I use this to make sure that:

1 When I take the putter back it tracks slightly inside the line

2 As the putter head strikes the ball the clubface is completely square.

On the way through the PathFinder, the putter head passes between the forward pegs slightly on an inside line. The putter head only just passes between the magnetized pegs and if I'm fractionally off line the peg's get pinged off. You don't have to set it up as severely as I do, there are many settings to accommodate any size of putter head and any ability of player.

The old fashioned mirror (below right) works wonders and I have had this one for years. It simply helps me check that my eyes are always over the top of the ball and that they haven't crept out of line.

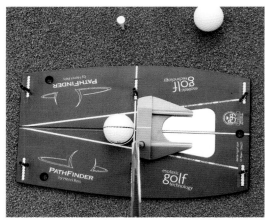

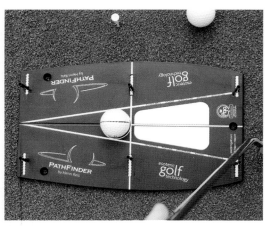

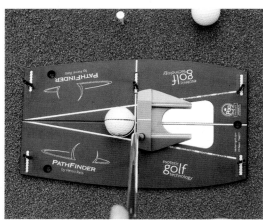

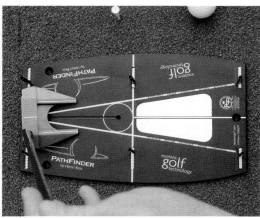

▲ A BIT OF FUN

I used to play this game with my brother growing up and now my son Luke likes to try and beat me. We find two holes on the putting green anywhere from 6 – 15 feet apart, normally with a little break in it. I stand at one hole and Luke stands at the other. The idea is that I have a go at putting into Luke's hole, and he will then get the chance to have a go putting at mine. If Luke holes the putt then he is one up. At this point we change sides and go again, the winner is the first person to get to five or ten depending on the length of putts you are trying. This game will give you a chance to whole out putts from right to left and vice versa, up and down hill in a fun but competitive way. It's something we do all the time.

I hope you have enjoyed this little insight as to how I approach holing out, and I honestly believe that if you spend some time practicing these drills, you will quickly improve and lower your scores.

Happy putting!
Ian Poulter

PLAYING
THE GAME OF GOLF

A SKYCADDIE FOR EVERY GOLFER

Accuracy you can afford

SPORT SERIES

AIRE   VOICE   GIMME   WATCH

TOUR SERIES

BREEZE   SGX   SGX^W

SKYCADDIE.CO.UK

Meet the family.

Which SkyCaddie to buy? The pocket-size Aire and Voice; the handy Watch; the classic big-numbers handset look of Gimme and Breeze; or the world-beating SGX and wireless SGXW?

They're all pre-loaded with SkyCaddie's ground-verified, professionally-mapped 30,000+ global course database – including over 99% of golf courses in Great Britain & Ireland. And because highly trained SkyCaddie mappers re-survey hundreds of golf courses each year, on foot, you can always be sure of accuracy. If it's not a SkyCaddie, you can't be certain. We're trusted by more serious golfers than all other rangefinders combined.

In 2013, don't buy something like a SkyCaddie. Buy a SkyCaddie.

 **SkyCaddie**®

#1 RANGEFINDER IN GOLF

ENGLANDGOLF
Official Rangefinder

PGA
The Professional Golfers' Association Partner
Official Rangefinder

PLOT YOUR
COURSE

In association with:

SkyCaddie®
www.skycaddie.co.uk

TIPS TO HELP YOU ACHIEVE YOUR LOWEST SCORE

210yds
190yds
175yds
165yds
150yds
140yds
130yds
120yds

1

Learn how far you hit the ball with each club, especially with the shorter clubs

Learning how far you hit the ball becomes easier to gauge as your technique improves, as you get a more reliable or predictable strike. As the consistency of strike improves you can start to monitor the distance that each club will, on average, travel. It is most important for you to get a total carry distance (how far the ball will travel through the air) as this is needed to see whether you will be able to get your ball over any obstacles on the golf course. By obtaining the carry number the total distance can be modified to whichever conditions the player may encounter; for example, a ball landing in the winter on soft ground will not roll as far as a ball landing on a dry fairway in the summer.

The short iron distances should have more precision as these are the scoring clubs. You should try to develop a favourite yardage that you are most comfortable with. This will help when we come to point 2.

SKYPRO™
SEE • GROOVE • IMPROVE

HOW DOES SKYCADDIE ENSURE 100% ACCURACY?

Of all the golf GPS brands, only SkyCaddie sends Tour caddie-trained Mappers to walk every single golf course with professional-grade survey equipment. SkyCaddie Mappers are very low handicap amateurs or pro golfers, walking on average 7.65 miles and recording c.2,500 sub-metre data points per 18-hole course map. That's almost 140 'distance markers' per hole, ground-verified to within 3 feet accuracy. SkyCaddie has mapped 30,000+ golf courses worldwide, including over 3,300 (99%+) in GB & Ireland. And only SkyCaddie re-walks hundreds of golf courses each year in the UK alone, when courses make changes. If it's not a SkyCaddie, your golf GPS map may well be out of date.

SKYCADDIE'S NEW SKYPRO – MAKING PRACTICE BETTER

SkyCaddie's new SkyPro (£169.95) swing analysis and training device launches in spring 2013 with the motto 'See, Groove, Improve'. It records and analyses golf swings you make during a practice session or lesson, and plays them back instantly on your smartphone or tablet. Named 'Best Product In Show' by Golf Monthly magazine on day 1 of the 2013 PGA Merchandise Show, the ultra-lightweight SkyPro clips to your golf club shaft, and Syncs via Bluetooth to the free SkyPro App. Ideal for solo practice, or golf lessons, SkyPro captures 100,000 data points per golf swing. "SkyPro will change the way teachers help golfers to improve" says world-famous golf coach Hank Haney.

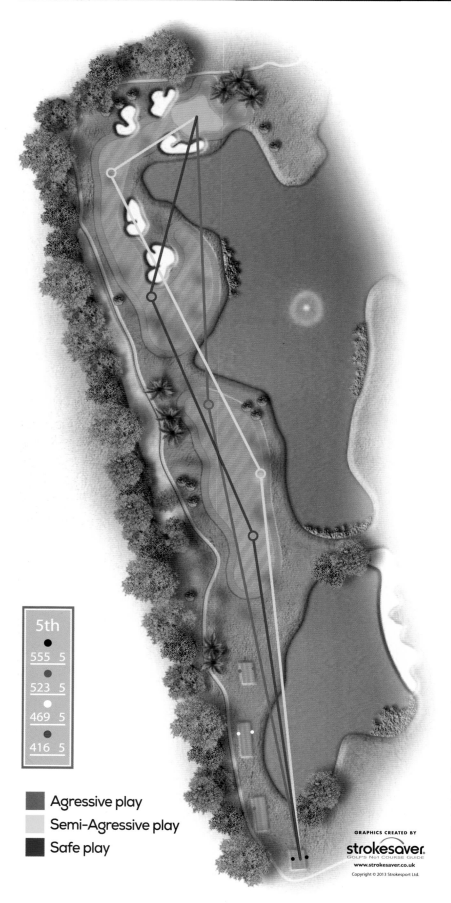

5th	
●	
555	5
●	
523	5
○	
469	5
●	
416	5

■ Agressive play
■ Semi-Agressive play
■ Safe play

GRAPHICS CREATED BY

strokesaver
GOLF'S No1 COURSE GUIDE
www.strokesaver.co.uk
Copyright © 2013 Strokesport Ltd.

2

Have a strategy for the hole ahead, but be prepared to modify this strategy when required

A strategy or plan will allow you to break the hole down into manageable chunks, rather than one daunting ordeal. Within this plan you should look at the layout of the hole and plan to hit to the wider parts of the fairway or to a position that will leave the easiest approach shot in. A long shot is often not the best option as this may be hitting to the narrowest part of the fairway or may leave an awkward shot from too close to the green. When you master point 1 you should utilise this information and play to leave your favourite shot if possible.

This strategy is not, however, set in stone. When the prior shot does not go as planned, which is inevitable at some point during the round, it is important to try not to make up for this mistake with your next shot. This could lead to more trouble and higher numbers. When you are in trouble such as bunkers, trees or long grass it is important to take your medicine and get the ball back in play.

3 Know your limits

Knowing your limits is crucial, so you don't try to play a shot that you haven't practised – it will very rarely come off. There is no harm in laying up short of a hazard if you don't think you can get over it. Remember 300 yards can be broken down into two 150 yard shots, and doesn't necessarily have to be tackled in one. Often the attempt to give your shot a little bit extra will end with you losing control of your ball, resulting in more shots.

Safe play

Agressive play

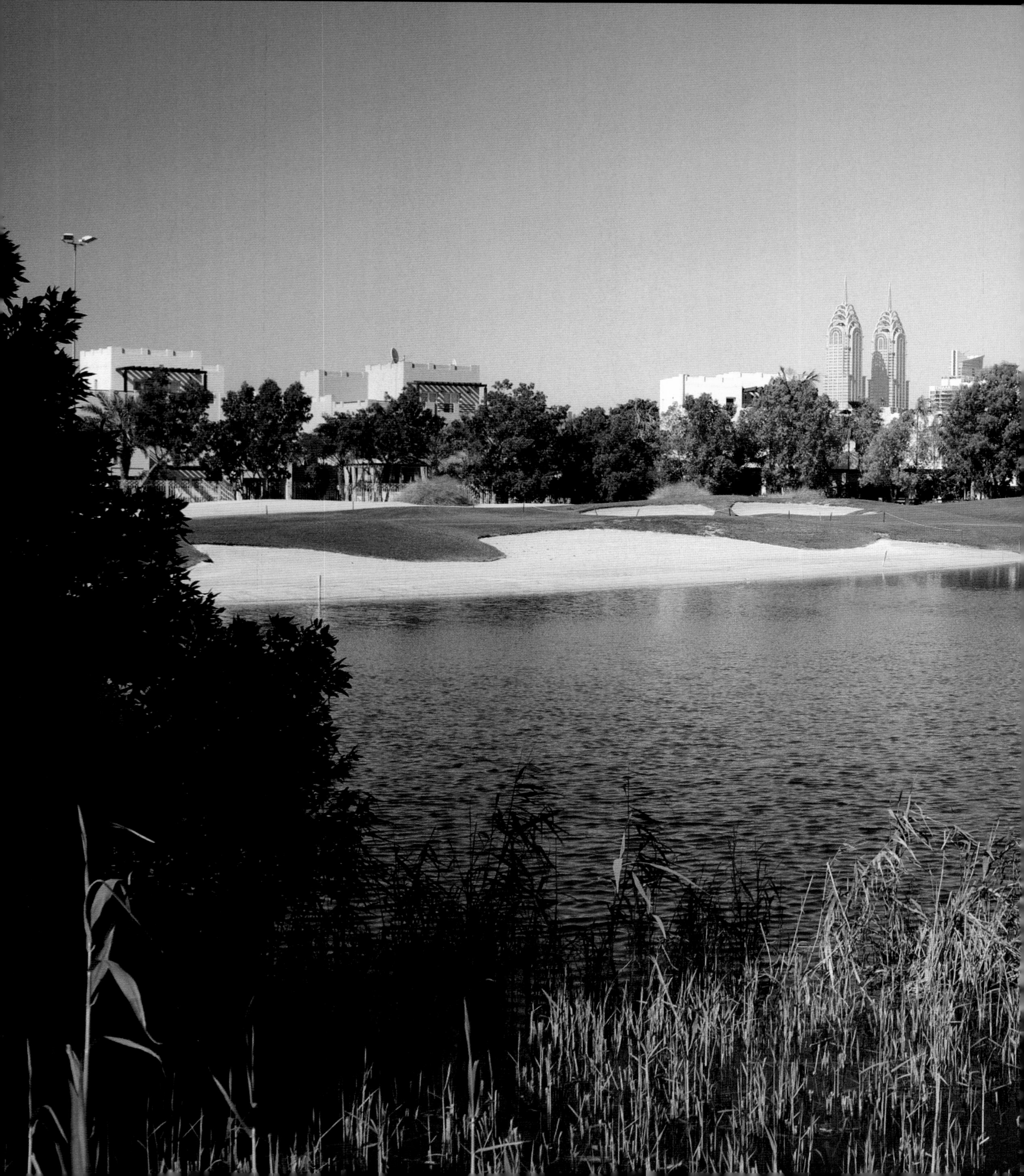

TOP TIP:
DON'T GET FLUSTERED

THERE'S ALWAYS A WAY OF SUCCESSFULLY TACKLING A HAZARD, SO KNOW YOUR YARDAGES, KEEP CALM AND EMPLOY THE HELP OF A SKYCADDIE

WHAT'S IN THE BAG?

Let's take a look inside the bag of a professional golfer – we can learn a lot from what they carry and the reasons why

CLUBS

As should you, the golf pro carries the maximum number of clubs allowed, which is 14. This tends to be broken down into the following groups:

> DRIVER

> 3 WOOD

> RESCUE CLUB

> 4 IRON – PITCHING WEDGE

> GAP WEDGE

> LOB WEDGE

> PUTTER

However, this can change depending on the course and conditions. If you were to play a links style course (where winds tend to blow hard) you should drop the rescue club and replace it with a 2 or 3-iron. This is because you need to keep the ball flight down because lynx courses are normally hard, with the ball regularly rolling a long way. If the course is playing short, you should drop the rescue club again, but this time replace it with an extra wedge. Ultimately, you'll only know what to carry once you have played a practice round and worked out your course strategy.

HIDDEN FROM VIEW

These are the bits and bobs you never get to see, but play just as important a role as the clubs

BALLS

Golf pros carry plenty of golf balls, not only because even they lose the odd ball, but also because during play the ball can get marked and scuffed, which directly affects its performance. Pros also use marker pens to individually mark their balls, making them easily identifiable. Pros all tend to play with similar makes of ball and sometimes hit the ball off line, so customising your ball is important. Mistaking (and playing) someone else's ball could result in penalty shots, and having to go back and play the shots again.

GLOVES

All golfers should carry four or five gloves. Why? Because during a round of golf, particularly if the conditions are hot, your hands will sweat – and the gloves tend to stretch out of shape. When playing in the rain it's also a good idea to take a few extra gloves, and use sandwich bags to keep them dry.

TEES AND BITS

Tees, pencils, pitch mark repairers and ball markers are an essential part of the kit and you should carry plenty of these.

FUEL

This is one of the most important items to have in your bag, but it's often the one amateurs tend to forget.

During a round of golf, pros will consume at least a litre of water as well as energy and rehydration drinks...it's crucial that you do the same.

You should also keep your body topped up with sugars and minerals during a round - pros will consume slow releasing sugars to keep them fuelled for the course. These generally take the form of fruits, nuts and energy bars – but not chocolate, which will give you a fast burst burn of energy that lasts for five to ten minutes, but not the constant gradual burn you need to last 3-4 hours.

COURSE MAPS & DEVICES

You should always carry a course yardage book with notes in (made during a practice round) along with a laser measuring device or GPS unit if you have one. We are always given a pin sheet (essentially a map of the green) for every round we play in tournaments, and the local rules sheet.

The PGA and European Tours don't allow measuring devices and lasers, so the pros have to rely on the old fashioned yardage books for all their information on yardages.

FIRST AID KIT

Not only is it important to carry a small first aid kit with you, but also consider carrying extra contact lenses, anti histamines and also sun block.

PLAYING IN THE RAIN

When playing in the rain (or if it's forecast for the day you hit the course) make sure you have at least one extra towel in your bag, along with a waterproof suit and umbrella. All golf bags come with a hood you should deploy before going out in the rain – you must keep your clubs as dry as possible.

THE ART OF GOOD PRACTICE

To get the best from your practice sessions, here are some handy tips and drills to ensure you get the most from your time on the golf course

1

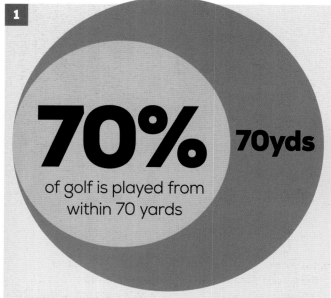

70%
70yds
of golf is played from within 70 yards

Your practice should reflect this, i.e. more short game practice than full swing. The short game is often referred to as the scoring zone, meaning this area is the simplest and most effective way to improve your score. It is very common to see the same swing problems that appear in the long game raise their head in the short, so working the short area more means you get more total game improvement, as your full swing game benefits along with improved scoring.

2 As human beings we prefer practising what we're good at – it's only natural. However, the game of golf is made up of lots of different parts and the best way to improve the total game is to work on your weak areas. It is no coincidence that the shot most golfers perceive as the hardest shot in golf (the 40 yard bunker shot) is also the least practised. If you have a weak area, don't brush it under the carpet, attack it head on. Your PGA professional can help you identify weak parts of your game, and improve them quickly.

3 The quality of your practice is more important than the amount of practice. Rather than rattle through a big bucket of balls, make sure you take your time in between shots. It is vital that you go through your pre-shot routine when you are practising – you don't hit two consecutive shots without moving off the spot on the course, so why do it in practice? It is important to change the club you are practising with as often as possible for the exact same reason.

5 DRILLS TO LIVE BY

1 *Make your practice reflect your play*

2 *Practice weaknesses, not strengths*

3 *Quality over quantity, every time*

4 *Drills or repetition = muscle memory*

5 *Some simple check points*

5 It is important to take care of some fundamentals when practising:

a. The first is to put a club or alignment stick on the ground, to ensure your club is aimed where you want the ball to start and your body is aligned parallel to your clubface.

b. To be consistent, you need to control where you strike the ground. Scratch a line in the earth, and use this as a reference as to where your club is hitting the grass. The better golfer will, more often, hit the ground after the line whereas the less experienced golfer will be striking the ground both sides of the line, or even missing the ground completely.

c. The strike is vital and off centre hits will produce an erratic shot pattern. By using strike tape the player can tell where the ball is hitting the face and this will help your PGA pro to diagnose any swing problems.

4 To improve technique it is important to get repetition of the correct movement which is often referred to as a drill swing. To make sure you are practising the correct movement be sure to contact your local PGA professional and seek advice on what to work on. Big changes need lots of repetition before they become natural, therefore it is vital to have a set of specific drills that you can practice on the range and if possible at home in front of a mirror.

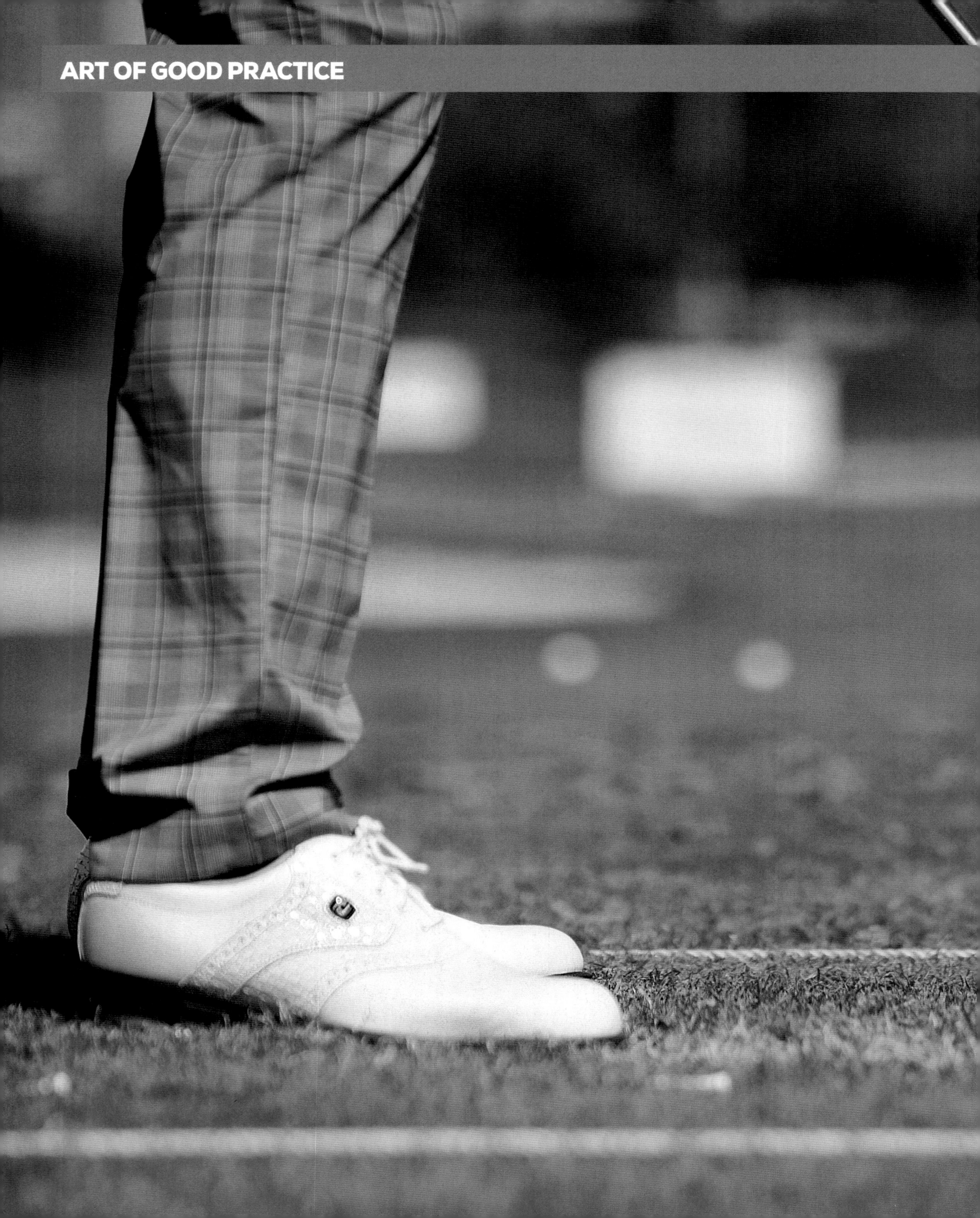

TOP TIP:

DRIVING RANGE

IF YOU LIVE IN A BUILT UP AREA, A GREAT PLACE TO PRACTISE YOUR GOLF IS YOUR LOCAL DRIVING RANGE

WHEN IT RAINS

Playing in the rain is not only unpleasant but, for obvious reasons, doing so makes it difficult to keep you and your equipment dry – crucial if you're to perform at your best. But for die-hard golfers who play in competitions (where there's no choice but to play, regardless of the weather), here are a few helpful tips.

Keeping Yourself Dry

This is half the battle, and failing to do so remains one of the main reasons for abandoning a round prematurely.

- Always carry an umbrella. You never know what the weather has in store for your round

- Make sure you have a good waterproof suit, and don't be afraid to splash a little extra cash on a high-quality product – when the rain starts you won't regret it. There are a broad variety of outfits available, ranging from merely splash proof right up to 100% waterproof and breathable. Take into consideration your golf course's climate to aid your purchase. A good suit will cost you the same price as a new driver, but you can be sure the investment is worth it.

Keeping Your Equipment Dry

Keeping your equipment dry is the hardest thing to do (but also the most crucial). Because you swing the club in the rain, water will sit on any head or shaft exposed and before long you will find your grips soaked, and that you can't keep hold of the club anymore. Here are a few tips to keep your equipment dry:

› Always carry spare towels, and introduce a fresh one every nine holes

› Make sure you have your bag's hood cover with you at all times

› Dry your clubs properly before putting them back in the bag

› Wedge tee pegs in the bottom of the grips, this raises the club ends off the base of the bag, where water can collect

Kit

There are a hundreds of products on the market designed to keep you and your equipment dry, try these:

› **Rain glove**. Amazingly these have only hit the market recently. All major manufacturers produce them, and the wetter they get the stronger they grip

› **Waterproof shoes**. All footwear companies produce waterproof shoes and many come with a three-year guarantee

› **Bag covers**. You can buy bag covers in most professional shops. They are 100% waterproof and cover the whole bag (unlike bag hoods). Most people have lightweight bags which are not waterproof. Conveniently, most bag covers fold down to the size of a 12 pack of golf balls

3 GOLDEN RULES

Focus on your pre-shot routine.

When playing a round of golf in the rain, taking time to prepare your shot makes all the difference (there's always a tendency to rush in poor weather). You may even find, as you take more care over your routine, that you play better in the rain. The extra concentration on making good swings while focusing on trying to hit more percentage shots quickly pays dividends.

1 *If you have chunky waterproofs on, make sure you fully complete the backswing. Do plenty of practice swings to get used to the extra layers*

2 *Always keep the clubface dry, and wipe it after every practice swing. If you don't, you will get a layer of water on the clubface, which will affect (negatively) how the ball flies and how far it goes*

3 *Remember when on the putting green that even a rain shower will cause the greens to run slower, and they will also break or turn less. Be firmer and straighter with your putting*

COURSE ETIQUETTE

These tips will help you and your fellow golfers enjoy your time on the golf course

"Golf is played, for the most part, without the supervision of a referee or umpire. The game relies on the integrity of the individual to show consideration for other players, care for the course and to abide by the Rules. All players should conduct themselves in a disciplined manner, demonstrating courtesy and sportsmanship at all times, irrespective of how competitive they may be." The R&A, the game's governing body

A FEW SIMPLE THINGS TO CONSIDER WHEN GOING TO PLAY A ROUND OF GOLF

1. Be on time. If you book a tee time make sure you arrive well ahead of it. Not only do you need to allow time for signing in and paying green fees, but also getting changed and sorting out your equipment.

2. Dress code. Make sure that you check when you book what the dress code is as it could cost more for the day than just your green fee.

3. Mobile Phones. The majority of clubs around the world have banned the use of mobile phones both on the golf course and in the clubhouse, but most allow you to use your phone in the car park.

4. Pace of Play. The pace of play is always important, and you should aim to play a round of golf in around four and a half hours. A good idea is to always keep up with the group ahead of you. If you are falling behind, there is no shame in letting the group behind you play through.

5. Out of Bounds or Lost Balls. It is always advisable to play a provisional ball from the tee if you think the ball could be lost. This means you won't have to return to the tee later (or wherever you played the shot from) if you can't find the ball.

6. Course Care. You should always leave the course how you would expect to find it. Always replace your divots and repair your pitch marks, and always rake the bunkers once you have finished in them. All rubbish must be placed in a bin on the course or taken back to the clubhouse for disposal.

7. Be Respectful to Other Golfers. Keep noise to a minimum. Shouting and outlandish behaviour can be off putting to other golfers and will not be tolerated by the club owners and management. In some cases it will result in you being asked to leave.

DRESS
CODE

Most golf courses around the world have a strict dress code which you must adhere to. Playing in jeans and a T-shirt is definitely frowned upon.

Here is a simple guide to what you should wear, and what you shouldn't if you want to avoid a pricey trip to the club shop.

Must have:
A collar, polo shirt tucked in, tailored trousers, soft spiked or studded golf shoes.

Must avoid:
Sleeveless T-shirt, beach or swim wear, jeans, sandals or training shoes.

IT'S ALL IN THE
NUMBERS

> " I spend a lot of time working and thinking about how to improve my game, but probably not as much time in the gym as I should. From experience, I know the importance of slow release energy as well as a host of other nutrients that can aid focus and physical performance. "

9
hours spent working behind a desk

3
nights spent working out in the gym

18
holes spent working on improving my game

If you'd like some specific advice on how proper nutrition could improve your physical state whilst on the course, email **golf@reflex-nutrition.com**

reflex®
Tomorrow's Nutrition Today™

ESSENTIAL WARM UP USING THE
GOLFBAND

The warm-up is one of the most important components of a healthy golf career. It is something many of us acknowledge but few of us do particularly well. Swinging a golf club requires flexibility and power, and it is important to prepare your body for this impact by completing golf-specific warm up exercises before taking your first swing. By the time tour professionals step to the first tee, they are fully prepared to make their best swings from the opening tee shot.

In order to reach your peak performance on the course, without injury, you must prepare physically before playing. Warming up before a game will enhance flexibility, help prevent injury and improve your game. The process of warming up increases blood flow to the muscles, encourages tight muscles to be stretched and lengthened, decreasing the chance of pulling and straining them and

also helps to achieve optimum swing performance. An effective golf warm up concentrates on muscles and movements which are specific to the sport. It would ideally include light cardio vascular and dynamic movements to get the heart rate up and blood flowing (i.e. a gentle jog or brisk walk), static stretches and golf swings. It should also focus on any problem areas i.e. shoulders and a stiff lower back. A good target is 10-25 minutes.

Prehabilitaion routines involve strength and conditioning exercises for specific muscles that help to reduce injury risk, before an injury actually occurs. Specific golf prehabiliation exercises concentrate on common injuries and strength imbalances, which occur due to the nature of the movements involved. Back pain is very common in golfers and a good warm up is one of the four key areas for its prevention, alongside

TOP TIPS

1. A good golf warm up exercise routine will prepare you physically and mentally for a strong performance on the golf course. Players who perform golf warm up exercises before playing tend to play better than if they've skipped warming up.

2. Not only should you take more time to get warmed up and stretch before practice or a round of golf, ideally you should do more stretching, flexibility and golf specific strength conditioning work at home.

swing technique, biomechanics and not carrying the golf bag. Going straight from the car directly to the tee and striking the ball as hard as possible is the easiest way to sprain back muscles, resulting in lower back pain.

Golf also places a large amount of stress on the arm and shoulder muscles. Shoulders need to be strong and injury free as they help support the swing, control the club and aid the follow-through. These GolfBand exercises below will help to warm up the rotator cuff muscles surrounding the shoulder joint, the chest and back, and core muscles in preparation for the game. You can choose to anchor the GolfBand to a securely fixed object or get someone to hold it as illustrated. To warm up the muscles and not exhaust them, use a medium-strength band, keep the repetitions low and keep the movement controlled and fluid with each full movement taking 2-3 seconds.

INTERNAL ROTATION
(shoulder, internal rotator cuffs)

> Stand sideways to an anchored GolfBand (at waist height)

> Stand with your feet shoulder width apart, keep a neutral spine and abdominals tight

> With your left hand hold the band with elbow bent at 90 degrees

> Throughout the exercise keep the elbow into the side of your waist and shoulder away from your ear

> Rotate your arm inwards so that your left hand comes across your body

> With control return to the starting position

> In a fluid motion repeat this motion 8-10 times before performing with your right arm

EXTERNAL ROTATION
(shoulder, external rotator cuff)

> Stand sideways to an anchored GolfBand (at waist height)

> Stand with your feet shoulder width apart, keep a neutral spine and abdominals tight

> With your right hand hold the band with elbow bent at 90 degrees

> Keep your elbow into the side of your waist & shoulder away from your ear

> Rotate your arm outwards then with control return it to the starting position

> Repeat this motion 8-10 times then perform with your left arm

ANTERIOR ROTATION
(shoulder, rotator cuff)

> Stand with your back to the anchored GolfBand (at waist height)

> Stand with your feet shoulder width apart, keep a neutral spine and abdominals tight

> Hold the band with your elbow bent at 90 degrees

> Keep your elbow in line with your shoulder joint and wrist straight

> Rotate your shoulder by pulling your hand down by 90 degrees until it's in-line with your shoulder

> Return to the starting position and repeat with a fluid motion 8-10 times

> Repeat with your opposite arm

POSTERIOR ROTATION
(shoulder rotator cuff)

> Stand facing the anchored GolfBand (at waist height)

> Stand with your feet shoulder width apart, keep a neutral spine and abdominals tight

> Hold the band with your elbow bent at 90 degrees

> Keep elbow in line with shoulder joint, wrist straight and forearm parallel with the floor

> Rotate your shoulder by pulling hand up by 90 degrees until your fist is pointing upwards

> Return to the starting position and repeat with a fluid motion 8-10 times

> Repeat with opposite arm

STANDING ROW
(upper back muscles, traps, lats and rhomboids help control the backswing and keep a good posture during the swing)

- Anchor the middle of the GolfBand (at waist height)
- Stand facing the band with your feet slightly wider than shoulder width apart, and knees bent slightly
- Hold the ends of the band in each hand, lean forward slightly, keep your head in-line with your spine and abdominals tight
- Start with your arms extended & elbows bent slightly
- Keeping your elbows close to your body, pull your elbows back squeezing your shoulder blades together
- With control return to the starting position and repeat 10-12 times

BACKSWING SWING DRILL
(warms up the core, shoulders and arms, and promotes full extension and width in the back swing)

- Stand in address stance, keep neutral spine and abdominals tight
- Secure the GolfBand on the ground to your left (to your right if left handed)
- This can be secured under your left/right foot or secured to a fixed object. (if no caddy or playing partner is free)
- Hold the band in both hands and slowly take the band back to replicate your backswing, hold at your full extension briefly before returning to the starting position
- Repeat with a controlled fluid motion 8-10 times

CHEST FLY
(chest, pectorals)

- Anchor the middle of the GolfBand (at shoulder height)
- Stand with you back to the band, feet slightly wider than shoulder width apart, and knees bent slightly
- Hold the ends of the band in each hand, lean forward slightly, keep your head in-line with your spine and abdominals tight
- Start with your arms out to the side and elbows bent
- Keeping your elbows soft, extended your arms forward and down bringing your hands together so your fists meet at arm's length in front of your thighs
- With control return to the starting position and repeat 10-12 times

FOLLOW-THROUGH DRILL
(warms up the core, shoulder, arms and pelvis, and will help strengthen your swing on impact).

> Stand in address stance, keep neutral spine and abdominals tight

> Secure the GolfBand on the ground to your right (to your left if left handed)

> This can be secured under your left/right foot or secured to a fixed object. (if no caddy or playing partner is free)

> Hold the band in both hands and create tension in the band

> With extended arms pull the band from low to high through the impact zone using lower and upper body rotation together

> Briefly hold the finish with your arms extended at shoulder height before returning to the staring position

> Repeat with a controlled fluid motion 8-10 times

A full warm up should also include legs, (specifically hamstring which are vital in setting up your golf posture), lower back, and gluteal muscles. The GolfBand programme provides a comprehensive range of stretches, warm up and strength training drills to improve your strength, balance, flexibility and power.

GolfBands are available from leading retailers, pro shops and:

www.golfband.co.uk

Spring all year round...

Cartilage and bone health are important for long term wellbeing and an active life. If you are looking for a daily supplement to give you extra support from within, *Jointace*® range has been specially formulated by Vitabiotics' experts to provide premium nutritional care. With a unique combination of nutrients, and vitamin C which contributes to normal collagen formation for the normal function of bone and cartilage.

Jointace nutritional support for an active life

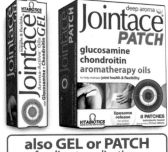
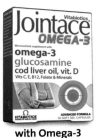
Original

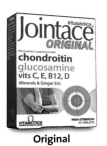
with Omega-3

Collagen

Max

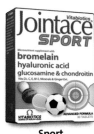
Sport

Fizz

also GEL or PATCH
for direct application.
Ideal alongside *Jointace*® Tabs or Caps.

From  , Superdrug, supermarkets,
Lloydspharmacy, chemists, Holland & Barrett,
GNC, health stores & *www.jointace.com*
Vitamin supplements may benefit those with nutritionally inadequate diets.

Voted Favourite
Supplement in its class
by Boots Customers

Most **loved** vitamins as voted by you

Britain's leading supplements
for specific life stages

Ω **VITABIOTICS**
SCIENCE OF HEALTHY LIVING

FAST FUEL

Eat well and carry right - the secrets to a good game. You park you car on a sunny, fresh morning. You open your boot, throw your bag over your shoulder and walk slumped into the clubhouse for your pre-round bacon sarnie and a cup of coffee. Is this the best way to start your golfing day?

You spend hours and hours perfecting your golf swing, however is it your nutrition that's letting you down?

BEFORE YOU LEAVE THE HOUSE
As with other sports, nutrition and hydration are extremely important in golf. A lack of food and low hydration levels lead to lack of concentration, poor motor control and muscle fatigue. To ensure you're in optimal shape for the course, it's important you're well fed and properly hydrated before you even leave for the golf course.

With only a small amount of effort you can create a meal that includes whole, fresh, nutritious food to ensure you're getting all the basic nutrients in the balance and form you need to perform at your best. This includes a combination of:

> **Proteins**
> **Carbohydrates**
> **Fats**
> **Vitamins**
> **Minerals**

GAME DAY
We now need to look at game day, and how to keep your energy levels up. I often spend time with golfers on improving their back 9-game, as stamina starts to ebb, and regardless of how much time you spend practising your short game and putting, muscle fatigue can play a huge factor in your energy levels. It's not rocket science, but eating as you play will keep your energy levels elevated and ensure muscle function and accuracy remains as strong as possible.

Plan to eat every two hours using a variety of ready-made snacks. These are easily carried and contain the extra boost required. Things like jerky, nut mix, energy bars and good old-fashioned sandwiches do the job perfectly.

Decreasing performance on the back-9 might also be a result of dehydration, and regular sips of water or a sports drink might help take your game to the next level. Both physical performance and neurological function are impaired by dehydration; so make sure you take on plenty of fluids before, during and after your round of golf.

So, what should you drink in advance to ensure you arrive at the first tee fully hydrated? Choose fruit juices, bottled water or herbal teas. Alcohol, excess tea and coffee should all be avoided, as

these are a diuretic. Another tip – odd as it may sound – is to eat your water. Snacking on fruit, which has a high water content, is an ideal way of doing so.

Make your liquid intake regular - you should begin drinking before you get thirsty. If you do feel the thirst coming on, I'm afraid you're a bit late. It's also important to take sips rather than gulping, as a large liquid intake flushes the kidneys causing very little absorption and leaving the body still craving the hydration it needs.

If you've finished panicking about whether you've taken on enough liquids, aren't chewing on an apple and have successfully avoided any water hazards, you're probably going to be lumping your clubs around on your shoulder. From a back-care point of view, this is terrible.

ENDURANCE
The body is a highly tuned machine, but it isn't designed to carry a heavy bag of golf clubs at an awkward angle for hours on end. In fact, lugging all those clubs around will have a detrimental effect on how your body performs during your round. Muscles will be shortened and tightened, creating muscular imbalances and this causes issues with muscle sequencing and balance. We spend hours practicing and perfecting our game, yet on game day we put our bodies through hell and then ask them to perform. Pain often comes along, which will not only cause mental distraction but will also impinge on movement.

In an ideal world we would all have caddies, but the next best thing is an electric trolley, a device that will enhance your endurance on the golf course handsomely. By using these we can eliminate the potential for muscle shortening and tightening, and reduce unneeded calorie expenditure. An electric trolley will also save your body from any postural problems it would normally incur from carrying a golf bag.

In summary, golf is hard enough without us allowing simple things like food, dehydration and back pain to make it tougher. Think and tune in to what your body is telling you and, more importantly, what it is asking for.

TOP TIPS

> Eat two hours before your tee off time to allow digestion. Look at creating a balanced meal the night before, hitting the main food groups.

> Drink plenty of fluid before your round and during the round sip frequently on water or a sports drink. Unfortunately, alcohol doesn't count.

> Go through a thorough warm up routine as described on the previous pages to wake up your muscles.

> Be aware of your posture during the round, use trolleys and buggies where possible.

> Fully hydrate after your round.

X7 Lithium

Fully remote controlled from 50m, available in 4 stunning colours and now with a lightweight lithium battery as standard, there has never been a better time to go remote.

The F1 Lithium

The unique feature of the remote controlled F1 Lithium is that it has a golf bag integrated into it's design, which allows the chassis to fold much smaller than the X7 (40% less volume and two thirds of the floor space).

Each F1 golf bag houses the handle of the trolley, and the three part chassis is designed to fold in one motion with no clips or latches.

The Z3 Push

With its great looks & full features list, it's easy to see why the Z3 Push has become the #1 selling trolley in stores up and down the UK.

STEWARTGOLF
DREAM MACHINES

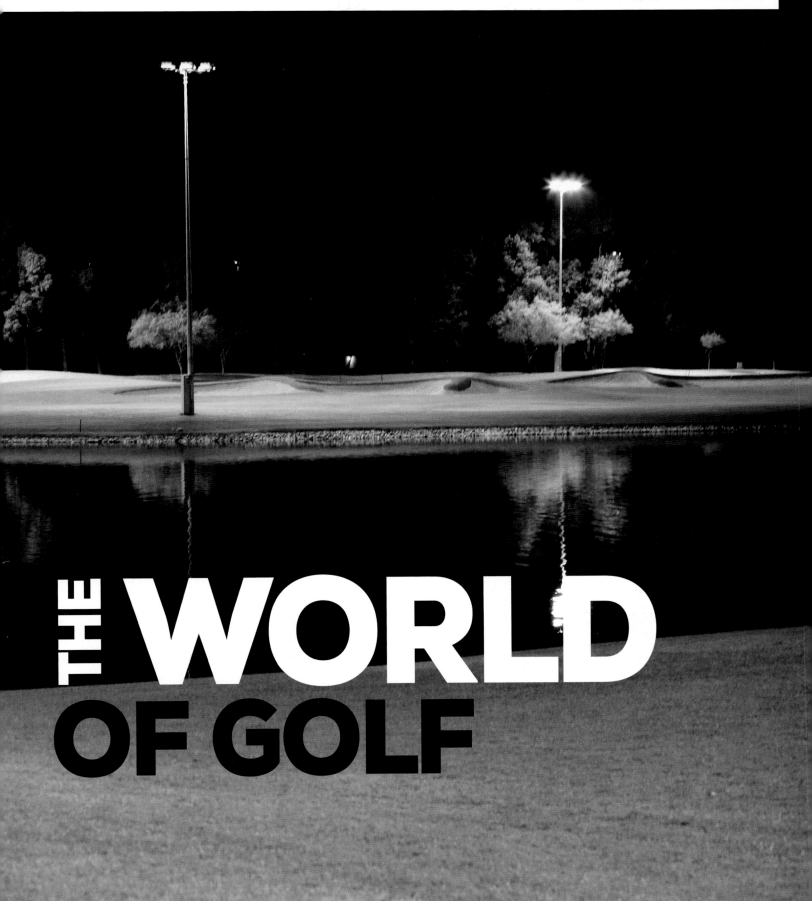

THE WORLD
OF GOLF

GOLF GOVERNING BODIES

GOLF'S GOVERNING BODIES

There are a number of governing bodies in the game of golf. Between them they set all of the rules of play along with the regulations regarding legality of your equipment.

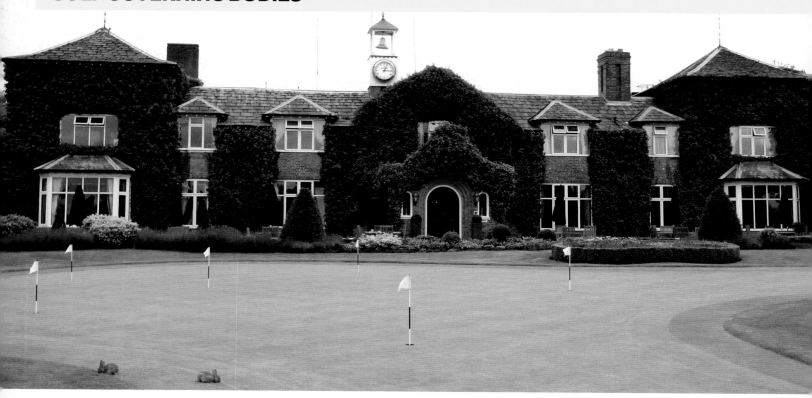

PGA

The PGA is a members' organisation for golf professionals. It has been at the heart of the game since 1901, when professionals of the day, led by the Great Triumvirate of JH Taylor, Harry Vardon and James Braid formed an organisation to protect the professionals' interests and promote the game of golf.

Now based at Centenary House at the famous Belfry, scene of four Ryder Cups, the Association is flourishing with more than 7,000 members.

Most are club professionals specialising in the core subjects of coaching and retailing, but increasing numbers are occupying managerial roles within golf clubs and resorts, both at home and overseas.

The PGA is dedicated to training and serving golf professionals whose principal aim is to offer a highly professional service to amateur golfers at a club, driving range or other golf establishment.

The PGA aims to gain the highest possible standards of employment for its members and therefore members must be highly trained, extremely competent and able to take on the complete role of professional or director of golf at any golf establishment.

The PGA also plays a significant role at different levels, from junior coaching through to government level, where it is helping formulate and determine policy for the sport. This includes active involvement with the England Golf Partnership's Whole Sport Plan, Club Golf Scotland, Golf Development Wales, Junior Golf Ireland and the implementation of the UK Coaching Certificate for golf.

Over the last 40 years there have been significant changes, which included a major restructure of the PGA in 1984, when the tournament playing division separated completely to form the European Tour.

The PGA still retains close ties with the Tour and is a Ryder Cup partner as the trustee of the actual Ryder Cup trophy donated by Sam Ryder. Its European links are further strengthened through another Ryder Cup partner, the PGAs of Europe.

The PGA has seven regions in Great Britain and Ireland with regional offices in the East, West, South, North, Midlands, Scotland and Ireland.

TOP TIP:
THE BELFRY

THE HOME OF THE PGA –
EVERY GOLFER SHOULD TEST
THEIR SKILL ON THE MIGHTY
BRABAZON COURSE

THE R&A

The Royal and Ancient Golf Club of St Andrews was founded in 1754. Golf was played here without many rules until 1897, when a group of gentlemen sat down and put pen to paper drawing up the first official rules of the game. Over the next 30 years the rules were tweaked and added to and they were eventually invited to take control of all golf competitions at St Andrews and other courses.

The R&A run some of the biggest amateur and professional golf tournaments in the world, 11 in total, including the biggest and oldest golf championship event, The Open (see page 123). This championship is not only for the best professionals in the game but also includes a handful of the world's best amateurs. The R&A also hold international and local qualifying events so professionals and amateurs who are in the top 100 in the world can get the opportunity to participate. The Open is played around a roster of 9 links golf courses throughout mainland UK, but every five years they return to the home of golf St Andrews.

The R&A along with the USGA set the regulations for all of the golf manufacturers from the design, size and length of the clubs to the dimple sizes and the amount that the balls can be compressed.

The R&A presides over the world of golf with the exceptions of the USA and Mexico, which is governed by the USGA - The United States Golf Association, see opposite.

USGA

The United States Golf Association is the governing body of amateur golf in Mexico and the USA. Together with the R&A they make and enforce the rules of golf around the world. The USGA also runs the national handicap system and tests golf equipment and balls to make sure that they conform with the regulations and guidelines.

The USGA was founded in 1894 by a small number of clubs to resolve the dispute over the national amateur championship, as two clubs had declared that the winner of their championship was the national champion.

In 1895 the USGA held the first official amateur championship. The US Open Championship for both amateurs and professionals wasn't held until 1898.

From the five original members back in the late 1900s they now have a membership of nearly 10,000 golf clubs today.

The USGA administers 13 national championships, three of which are for professionals, including the US Open - one of the four prestigious annual majors.

EUROPEAN TOUR

The tour was run as a separate section of the Professional Golfers Association (PGA of Great Britain and Ireland).

As the tour grew in the mid 1970s the PGA decided to set up its players division based at Wentworth Golf Club in Surrey.

By 1984 the tour had grown so much, with more tournaments being added across mainland Europe that the tour needed to branch out on its own. So with the leadership of Neil Coles The European Tour was born. Over the next ten years the tournament players found themselves with over 30 tournaments to play in, some as far afield as Asia.

By 1995 the European Tour had branched out, and they now had many co-sanctioned events in Asia, South Africa and Australia. The schedule had now grown to 35 international events and the prize funds available were rapidly increasing year on year.

The European Tour has two other tours that it now administers:

The Challenge Tour, which sits under the main tour. This is where golfers develop both their skills and game, and if they finish in the top 20 at the end of the season they gain their full tour cards for the European Tour.

The European Seniors Tour, which is for the over 50s, founded in 1992 to give the older player the opportunity to still be competitive and play against players their own age.

PGA TOUR

The PGA Tour is the association and organiser of the men's main professional golf tours in the USA and North America.

It organises nearly all of the flagship tournaments in the USA except for three majors and the World Golf Championships (WGC) but still helps with referees and officials.

The PGA of America originally established the tour, but in 1968 the tour players separated from the club professionals and the PGA Tour was born.

In 2013 there are 34 tournaments on the schedule and this doesn't include the four WGC events and the four major championships.

Over the last 15 years the prize funds have increased dramatically due to growth in popularity of the game and exposure through the TV and media.

In 1992, Fred Couples played 22 events and won the order of merit with $1,344,188. In 2012, Rory McIlroy played 16 events and won the order of merit with $8,047,952.

The PGA Tour now has two other Tours:

The Web.com Tour, which is a development tour where the 25 players gain their playing rights on the main tour the following season:

The Champions Tour, where many of the legends of the game now over 50 get to carry on competing at a high level.

The PGA tour is very proud of its charity work and we personally know the players and their wives participate in helping out charities where tournaments are being played. The PGA Tour is very proud to have raised over $1 billion for charities around the country.

THE MAJORS

Every sport has its prestigious competitions, and golf is no different. Golf's premier competitions are called Majors, and there are four held each year; three in the USA and one in the UK. They are the biggest golf tournaments in the world and offer the highest prize money, so it's no surprise that you get the biggest names slogging it out for the top honours.

THE US OPEN

This year the US Open will be played at Merion Golf Club in Pennsylvania. It will be the fourth time the club has hosted the competition, but the first time it has been played on the East Course. The previous three times the club has hosted the competition, it has been played on the West Course, with the venue first used for the championship in 1934.

The US Open is administered and organised by the USGA (see page 117) which has a large number of clubs keen to hold the event. It is the set up of the courses that makes this championship special. Extremely narrow fairways with rough so deep that even if you're lucky enough to find your ball you'll have a tough job hacking it back on to the fairway. The rough also continues around the greens, making chipping and pitching extremely hard.

By doing this the USGA puts the focus on long straight hitting from the tee, and accuracy with shots into the greens. Very rarely will you see 16 under par totals winning the event as Rory McIlroy did back in 2011, just above and below par is normal.

They have similar qualifying criteria as The Open (see page 123) and amateurs also get the opportunity to win a place in this prestigious tournament.

One rule that separates the US Open from other championships is that there is no sudden death playoff if there's a tie after four rounds. Instead, there is a fifth day of play and the players that are tied play a further 18 holes to determine the winner. Only if they are still tied after Monday's play will they go into sudden death, but this has only ever happened three times.

This year the winner's cheque will be for over $1.4 million and a total prize fund of $8 million. Not bad for a week's work...

The Ryder Cup

This biennial golf competition is played between 12 of the best American and 12 of the best European golfers, over three days of intense golf. The venue alternates between the US and Europe and has been played on some of the most famous golf courses in the world.

The Ryder Cup started after an exhibition match between members of the British PGA and American professionals at Wentworth Golf Club (Surrey) in 1926. The following year the Ryder Cup was officially played in Massachusetts in the US at Worcester Country Club.

The Ryder Cup itself was donated and named after Samuel Ryder, a Hertfordshire entrepreneur, and the golden trophy is the only prize – the participants play for pride and bragging rights alone.

Originally only British professionals took part, but in 1973 the Republic of Ireland was officially included. In 1979 US domination led to the tournament opening up to the rest of Europe, and since then the Ryder Cup has been a much more closely contested competition. The Europeans have won seven of the last nine matches and they haven't lost a match on European soil since 1993.

THE US PGA CHAMPIONSHIP

The PGA of America is responsible for this tournament, and up until 1957 it was a match-play championship. With pressure coming from TV broadcasters looking for bigger names playing in the final few rounds, the PGA relented and changed it to a 72-hole stroke-play event.

The PGA Championship was established for the purpose of providing a high-profile tournament specifically for professional golfers. In the early days professionals were not held in high regard, and golf was originally a sport run largely by wealthy amateurs. This origin is reflected in the entry system for the US Championship. It is the only major which does not explicitly invite leading amateurs to compete (it is possible for amateurs to get into the field, although the only viable way is by winning one of the other major championships). It is also the only championship which reserves a large number of places, 20 of 156, for club professionals. These slots are determined by the top finishers in the club pro championship, held in June.

THE OPEN

This is the oldest of the four majors and is the only major played outside the USA.

Administered by the R&A and always played on a links golf course this tournament is always played in third week of July.

They are playing for the trophy called the Claret Jug, first awarded back in 1873 to Tom Kidd of Scotland and he won the princely sum of £11. In 2012 Ernie Els of South Africa won the trophy and his reward was £900,000.

The Open rotates the courses its plays and there are currently 9 courses on the schedule but every five years the championship returns to the home of golf, St Andrews.

Tour professionals and highly ranked amateurs that are exempt are able to take a chance and enter through one of five international final qualifying competitions played over 36 holes. The 28 places available are divided amongst Asia, Australasia, Africa, America and Europe.

The rest of the field - normally 12 places - is made up from hundreds of amateurs and professionals playing through regional and local qualifying stages to get the chance to play on the big stage.

This year the tournament will take place in Scotland at Muirfield Golf Club near Gullane. This year will be quite special as Ernie Els will be defending his title and he was the last winner of The Open at Muirfield back in 2002.

The field is made up of 156 players broken down in to the following categories:

Around 115 of the players are made up of
> Top 50 in the world
> Top 10 from last year's event
> Winners of the three other major for last 5 years
> Past winner under the age of 60
> Top 30 on the previous year's PGA & European Tour order of merits

PLAYER

WELL PLAYED ERNIE SEE YOU AT MUIRFIELD 2013

TheOpen.com

COURSES IN SCOTLAND:

> The Old Course St Andrews
> Carnoustie Golf Links
> Muirfield
> Turnberry
> Royal Troon

COURSES IN ENGLAND:

> Royal St Georges
> Royal Birkdale
> Royal Lytham & St Annes
> Royal Liverpool (Hoylake)

THE MASTERS

The Masters is the first major championship of the season, played at Augusta National Golf Club, a private members golf club in Georgia, USA. The Masters was the brainchild of Clifford Roberts and the legendary amateur golfer Bobby Jones - the only golfer to complete the grand slam of golf, winning all the major tournaments in a single season.

The tournament is traditionally played in the first full week in April.

Bobby Jones designed the golf course along with famous course architect Alister MacKenzie, and they were truly blessed with the landscape and terrain. The land was a plantation and early nineteenth century plant nursery, and work began in 1931 with the official opening in 1933.

The course is probably one of the most physically and mentally demanding courses they play, with huge elevation changes alongside severely sloped, fast greens.

The greens at Augusta are some of the largest surfaces on tour but are without doubt the hardest greens to read and putt on due the sheer severity of slopes and pace that they are able to get them running at. It's not uncommon to see players putting with their backs to hole and hitting balls some 30 feet away from the hole in order to watch the roll back towards the hole.

The Masters was first played 1934 and the field was made of Bobby Jones's close friends and associates.

It is the only major where there is a limited field of around 90 players, comprised of the top 50 players in the world, past winners and invitations.

The halfway cut in this tournament is different to the other majors, where normally the field is cut to the top sixty and ties. The Master has a cut for top 44 and those players that are within 10 shots of the leader.

The winner of the tournament receives the coveted Green Jacket from last year's winner and has it presented to him in the Butler Cabin soon after the tournament has ended. The presentation is then repeated close to the 18th green in front of all of the spectators. The jacket is worn by the members of the club and past winners, but the jackets are only to be worn at the club and must never leave the grounds of the club - a few of them have managed to sneak it out, only for them to be returned soon after.

The winner also receives a gold medal and a silver miniature version of the trophy, which is a huge replica of the clubhouse. This tournament has many traditions and here are just a few of them:

The Champion's Dinner is always held on the Tuesday evening before the tournament starts. The defending champion gets to set the menu and all the past winners of the tournament are invited for dinner.

The Par 3 Contest is held on Wednesday afternoon and is a bit of fun for the players, many of whom have their children, family and friends caddying for them. It's not a contest they are trying to win as, to date, no winner of The Par Contest has ever gone on to win the main event.

Crystal. Players are awarded beautiful pieces of crystal for special feats in tournament:

Lowest score of the day: Crystal Vase
Hole In One: Large Crystal Bowl
Every Eagle: Pair of Crystal Goblets

THE RULES OF GOLF

Basic Rules Of Golf

Here are some of the basic rules of golf, with their corresponding rule number allowing you to quickly look up a ruling and determine whether you have incurred a penalty, or are entitled to free drop or relief.

Every golf club will have a small booklet of the rules published by the R&A that are free for you take. However, from time to time you will either forget the book or misinterpret a ruling – in this situation use Rule 33. Simply play the ball how it lies, then play a second ball under your own interpretation of the ruling and record both scores. You must then notify the competition organiser once you have finished play and let them make a final decision.

Always play the ball as it lies. Don't improve your lie, the area of your intended stance or swing, or your line of play by:

> Moving, bending or breaking anything fixed or growing, except in fairly taking your stance or making your swing

> Pressing anything down (Rule 13-2).

If your ball is in a bunker or water hazard, don't:

> Touch the hazard with your hand or club before your downswing

> Move loose impediments (Rule 13-4). All of these incur penalties and will add shots to your score if broken.

A MAXIMUM OF 14 CLUBS ALLOWED IN THE BAG

Carrying too many clubs will cost you two penalty shots for every hole you play, with a maximum penalty of four shots awarded if the infringement is not detected before the third hole.

The teeing ground
Tee Shot (Rule 11)

Play your tee shot from between, and not in front of, the tee markers.

You may play your tee shot from up to two club-lengths behind the front line of the tee markers.

If you play your tee shot from outside this area:

> In match play there is no penalty, but your opponent may require you to replay your stroke provided he does so immediately

> In stroke play you incur a two-stroke penalty and must play a ball from within the correct area

Bunkers

If your ball is in a bunker you may play the ball as it lies or take relief under a penalty one stroke, dropping the ball behind where the ball lay, keeping that point between where the ball lies and where you are dropping.

If you ground your club in the bunker or touch the sand with your club you will incur a penalty of two shots.

Hazards
Water Hazards (Rule 26)

If your ball is in a water hazard (yellow stakes and/or lines) you may play it as it lies or, under penalty of one stroke:

> Play a ball from where your last shot was played

> Drop a ball any distance behind the water hazard keeping a straight line between the hole, the point where the ball last crossed the margin of the water hazard and the spot at which the ball is dropped

If your ball is in a lateral water hazard (red stakes and/or lines), in addition to the options for a ball in a water hazard (see above), under penalty of one stroke, you may drop a ball within two club-lengths of, and not nearer the hole than:

> The point where the ball last crossed the margin of the hazard

> A point on the opposite side of the hazard equidistant to the hole from the point where the ball last crossed the margin

Lost Ball

Always put an identification mark on your ball; many golfers play the same brand of ball and if you can't identify your ball, it is considered lost (Rules 12-2 and 27-1)

Provisional Ball (Rule 27)

If your ball is lost outside a water hazard or out of bounds you must play another ball from the spot where the last shot was played, under penalty of one stroke.

You are allowed five minutes to search for a ball. If it is not found within that time, it is considered lost.

If, after playing a shot, you think your ball may be lost outside a water hazard or out of bounds you should play a provisional ball. You must state that it is a provisional ball and play it before you go forward to search for the original ball.

If the original ball is lost (other than in a water hazard) or out of bounds, you must continue with the provisional ball, under penalty of one stroke. If the original ball is found in bounds, you must continue play of the hole with it, and must stop playing the provisional ball.

FORMATS OF PLAY

THE **TWO MOST POPULAR** FORMATS ARE

Stroke Play or Medal Play

This is the purest form of the game, where every shot is counted and totalled at the end of the round. This is also the way your first handicap is assessed, and as your scores get lower as you improve, so will your handicap.

Match Play

This is played either on your own or in pairs. You play against another player or his team, and the aim is to win each individual hole, with the lowest score taking the hole.

MONTHLY MEDAL

This is a competition run monthly by clubs where every stroke you play is counted, and your handicap is adjusted at the end of the round. Clubs will adjust your handicaps after these tournaments and you will often need to play in at least three of these competitions during the year to keep your handicap alive. You will often find societies and corporate golfers using the Stableford format as it's a very forgiving format of play.

Stableford

This is a points-based system that can be played in a stroke play or match play format:

Albatross	(-3 under par)	5 Points
Eagle	(-2 under par)	4 Points
Birdie	(-1 under par)	3 points
Par		2 Points
Bogey	(1 over par)	1 Point
Double Bogey	**or worse**	0 points

Everyone has a bad hole or two in a round of golf and it doesn't matter if you run 10 up on a par three, you have only missed out on two points.

OTHER GAMES TO TRY

Four Ball

This is played in two teams formed of two players each. Each player will play their own ball for the entire hole, and the lowest of the two scores per team is taken as the team score.

Foursomes

In teams of two, players not only hit alternate shots until the hole is finished, but also alternate tee shots. Player one hits the odd number hole tee shots and player two takes the even number hole tee shots.

Better Ball

This is very similar to Four Ball, but here the teams can consist of up to four players. In each case, the lowest score made by any team member on a hole is counted as the team score.

Greensomes

This game is a slight variation of foursomes, the main difference being that in Greensomes both players hit a tee shot. The best shot is chosen and the other player will hit the next shot. The team will continue to hit alternate shots until holed out.

Texas Scramble

Here, teams can be made up to four players. Each player tees off, and the whole team takes their second shot from where the best tee shot landed. Again, the best shot is chosen and all players hit their next shot from this spot. The team continues in this fashion until the hole is completed. Sometimes, the use of a set number of tee shots from each team member is required.

Your local pub can be a great place to find a local golfing society.

GOLFING SOCIETIES AND CORPORATE GOLFING

There are over 2,500 golf courses in the UK and Ireland, and in tough economic times many of these clubs are struggling for members. This is because subscription golfers who only play a couple of times end up paying hundreds of pounds a round.

For many golfers this is just too expensive, meaning golf society, corporate, charity and even PGA Pro-am golf days are becoming both more popular and more fun to play in.

Arranging one of these days is not as daunting as you may think, and below we've put together a list of things you need to do to get your own society or corporate golfing day off the ground. Before you know it you and your friends will be playing some of the most beautiful golf courses around the country.

For many golf clubs, a golf society is based on 12 players or more. You will find that most golf clubs will not allow group bookings on a weekend, but there are a few that will allow weekend societies – or even permit a friendly four-ball booking.

Here's how to go about it
Set your budgets How much are you prepared to spend on a day's golf?

Consider:
Green fees
You will find that many clubs have competitive packages to offer, including breakfast, lunch or dinner with your golf. These packages offer you the best value for money, and help you to budget your golf day more easily.

Prizes
If you are arranging a corporate or charity day don't forget some after dinner entertainment or even a trick shot show.

What type of course?
Private members clubs. These are normally very accommodating during the week, but will tend to turn you down at weekends, when their members usually play.

Proprietary golf clubs
Again, very accommodating during the week but may be more inclined to allow you arrange a weekend day than private members clubs.

Public/municipal golf club
These are very busy courses and normally run by the borough councils. They are always open to societies and golf days but, arranging a weekend day will be difficult.

Handicap certificates
When choosing a course, always check with the club to see if your guests require handicap certificates. If they do, and some of your golfers have never been a member of a golf club and don't have a certificate, then they may not be allowed to play. However, if the majority of your members are competent golfers,the odd player without a certificate shouldn't be a problem...but it's always worth checking first.

Prizes are an essential part of a golfing society or corporate day
Always use the golf course's club professional and his club shop when you are buying prizes for your day. The Pros are always very helpful and, because they usually carry good stock, winners will be able to change sizes and colours at the event. The club pros will also arrange 'Nearest the Pin' and 'Longest Drive' challenges...and some of them will provide gift vouchers for the pro shop.

Try to give a selection of prizes, and always include awards for the worst dressed, worst shot and highest score on a hole. These all provide great entertainment at the prize giving.

All golf clubs will have an employee dedicated to supporting you in your needs. They will be ready to do as much organising as is needed to make your day go smoothly.

Do bear in mind that many clubs get booked up very quickly, so you must always try to book dates at least 6 months in advance if you want to play the best courses.

JUNIOR
GOLF

Junior golf has never
been in a healthier
state, and with junior
coaching programs
and the support of
the PGA and Golf
Foundation, the
future has never
looked brighter for
young golfers

Unfortunately, young golfers haven't always had this kind of support. There was a time when junior sections at many golf clubs were run by enthusiastic members, with little help from the clubs themselves. We were always restricted to the times we could play at, often after four o'clock at weekends during the summer and after two o'clock in the winter. This meant we often only had time to play nine holes, and if given time to play competitions we were hassled to stand aside and let adults play through. Juniors were considered a hassle to the members, and were banned from competing in men's competitions at some clubs until they were 18 years old – even if they had single-figure handicaps.

Thankfully attitudes have now changed, and the old-fashioned stuffiness of old has (largely) evaporated, with junior golfers now being treated as the lifeblood of the clubs, as indeed they are.

One of the biggest names in golf during the 1950s, Sir Henry Cotton (three-time Open Champion), and golf correspondent Henry Longhurst decided to take the game to the schools. Within a few short years golf was being taught in over 200 schools, and with the help of other coaching groups a total of

6,000 juniors were soon participating in the sport.

Since then, with the Golf Foundation's backing, the junior game has blossomed, and today over 150 junior tournaments are held at clubs all over country, producing some exciting players in the process.

Many of the world's top players show their support for grass routes golf. Lee Westwood, Rory McIlroy, Ian Poulter, Darren Clarke, Sir Nick Faldo, Tiger Woods and Ernie Els, to name a few, have their own junior foundations, and hold events all over the world to inspire young golfers with talent to progress in the game.

The PGA also supports programmes, and there are now over 2,000 golf courses and driving ranges around the country that hold junior coaching days in school holidays and at weekends, allowing you to take your child along for coaching. Most of the time you won't even need to be a member of a club or range - simply find your closest course and call them for information.

Golf in Britain hasn't been in ruder health for years, so turn over to see the three events and programmes supported by some of the best UK tour professionals.

DARREN CLARKE
GOLF SCHOOL

2011 British Open winner Darren Clarke is passionate about giving back to golf, a game that has given him so much.

The Darren Clarke Golf School opened its doors in September 2010 to young golfers (aged 16 and over) wishing to undertake a two year full-time course where they get the opportunity to enhance their game while receiving A-level equivalent qualification. Already the School has shown real success on the course, including previous students Alan Dunbar and Paul Cutler representing Great Britain & Ireland in the 2011 Walker Cup.

Darren is a regular visitor to the school, contributing priceless knowledge and experience. Through the school, children of all ages and abilities are given the opportunity to experience the great sport of golf. As part of Darren's ongoing commitment to supporting junior golf and cancer charities, the school is now assisting with delivery of the Darren Clarke Foundation coaching initiative. The main aim is to introduce the game of golf, for free, to young children in all parts of Ireland.

Clarke said: "I'm pleased with the progress of the initiative. Golf has been so good to me, so it's always been important to me to give something back. It's great that youngsters, who otherwise might not have the opportunity, are being given the opportunity to play this great game."

2013 has two new initiatives, the Darren Clarke Golf Tour and Darren Clarke Golf Camps. The Golf Tour offers junior golfers the opportunity to play on a tour, which will culminate with a Tour Players Championship Final.

www.darrenclarkegolfschool.com

LEE WESTWOOD
GOLF SCHOOL

You never forget a great teacher, and if you're lucky enough to really connect with one and take heed of what they have to say, it has the power to map out a future path to success.

Essentially, that is the mission at the Lee Westwood Golf School, which has centres located in the north and south of England and in Florida, USA, providing on-site facilities and coaching in golf and education.

In September 2010 the Lee Westwood Golf School first opened its doors in Cheshire with 22 excited young golfers beginning their two-year full-time course. With the support and partnership of Lee Westwood, his management ISM and sponsors, junior golfers are getting the opportunity to improve their game whilst receiving a first-class education. The school itself boasts a 100 percent retention rate, and students are typically achieving higher than the national average in their academic work.

In a short period of time the students have achieved some great results, including winning the 2012 British Schools & Colleges National Title. There have been a number of individual performances, notably Kieran Waters who gained international honours via English Schools National representation in 2012.

Lee has committed his team to driving junior golf forward in 2013 and has introduced two new initiatives, the Lee Westwood Golf Tour and Lee Westwood Golf Camps. The Lee Westwood Golf Tour will provide young golfers the opportunity to experience playing on a tour, similar to their golfing heroes, on selected golf courses around various areas of the UK.

www.leewestwoodgolf.com

IAN POULTER
INVITATIONAL

With the number of budding golfers growing in the UK, there's never been a better time for juniors to get into the sport. One golfer who has been leading the way in championing juniors for the last eight years is Ian Poulter, with the support of his golf clothing brand, IJP Design.

This year sees the eighth Ian Poulter Invitational in association with IJP Design and Woburn Golf Club take place in July. The tournament welcomes 100 rising junior stars from across the UK and around the world, to play on the challenging Marquess Course at Woburn Golf Club. Players, all of whom have to be under 18 years of age on the 1st January 2013 with a maximum 16 handicap to qualify, get rare one-on-one time with Ian as he tours the course to give hands-on professional guidance to each player, as well as top tips and practical advice during the afternoon's 'IJP Clinic'.

Ian says, "It's always such a special day to get some of the best junior golfing talent together and give them an opportunity I never had. I'm always incredibly impressed by the standard of the boys and girls competing and I love being out on the course with the kids, being able to chat with them and seeing their genuine enthusiasm for the game. It's a great experience for the juniors, always a really refreshing day for me and one I look forward to every year."

On the day, prizes are awarded for the best gross and net scores, as well as for 'Best Dressed' and 'Best Haircut' and this year the charity associated with the event is Dreamflight, whose purpose it is to send seriously ill children on the holiday of a lifetime.

www.ijpdesign.com

I WEAR
THE TROUSERS
DO YOU?

#WeartheTrousers

IJP DESIGN
JUNIOR COLLECTION
www.ijpdesign.com

CUSTOM FITTING

Whether you are looking to buy your first set of clubs, or simply want to upgrade your current set, it is always worth having a good look around to ensure you get the best value for your budget.

There are so many manufacturers out there with four or five different sets of irons, woods, wedges and putters to choose from that selecting the right set of clubs can be more than daunting. You will find manufacturers eagerly trying to flog you everything from bladed irons used by the scratch golfer and professional through to cavity-backed and hybrid clubs designed to be more forgiving on off-centre hits (i.e. for the beginner). You only need to go into your local pro shop to see the number of products available, and even they are limited to the brands they can carry due to the size of their shops. However, your local pro will be able to advise you on what they have in stock as well as other brands they are able to supply.

Over the last 80 years the PGA golf professional has trained in the art of custom fitting golf clubs, and in the early days were actually club makers and builders. They pride themselves on being able to offer golfers the best service and advise when it comes to selecting your golf equipment, understanding that no two golfers are alike, from physical shape through to size of budget.

Most golf club manufacturers now have full custom-fit services across their whole range of products, and your local pro will be able to correctly fit you a set of clubs (or arrange for you to visit one of the many custom-fitting centres around the country). It is essential you try as many clubs as possible before making a purchase, as the financial outlay is no small one – make sure you take your time to choose exactly the right clubs for you and don't be rushed. All manufacturers have demo clubs you can try on the practice ground, and during the summer many club pros arrange demo days for manufacturers to visit their clubs, demonstrate their wares with potential customers and carry out custom fittings.

All this means that these days you are able to buy a perfect fitting set of golf clubs, much like the tour stars. A little known fact is that 95% of the time manufacturers will not even charge you for this service. After all, it is in their best interests to enhance your enjoyment of the game by providing you with a correct fitting set of clubs.

WHICH CLUB TO BUY

Everyone is built differently, and the clubs available 'off the peg' will only fit about 5% of golfers playing the game today. Choosing the wrong clubs can actually make your game worse rather than better, so read on to find out what a club pro will look for when fitting you out.

SHAFT
SELECTION

There are hundreds of shafts available on the market, and they all have slightly different playing characteristics. From graphite to steel, out there somewhere will be a shaft that will help you hit the ball further, straighter and with more control.

When fitting, getting the correct flex in the shaft is the first thing a pro will aim to sort, as this will maximise your club head speed. This is rated from A flex, which is for ladies and seniors, to X flex, which is recommended for stronger golfers and tour professionals.

A shaft's kick point has the ability to make the ball fly higher or lower. The kick point is the place where the shaft flexes as you hit the ball, and having a high kick point (which is closer to the grip of the club) will help lower the ball's flight. A kick point nearer the head of the club will help get the ball airborne. Once you have the correct flex, playing around with the kick point will help you get the best from every club.

Torque in the shaft is also worth looking at, as it can reduce the amount of hook and slice on the ball. Torque is the amount the club head twists and resists through impact, and slicing the ball with a shaft that has high torque will make the club head release and close more during the swing. During a custom fitting, make sure to ask the pro the effect of torque specific to your own swing.

Shafts also vary in weights – especially graphite models, which are manufactured light to help increase your club head speed, feel and control. This will improve your distances, especially with the woods, but try to avoid graphite shafts in the irons, as this can affect your accuracy and distance control.

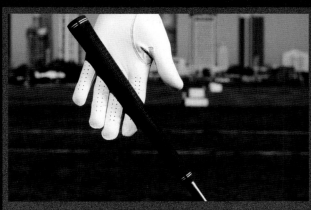

GRIP SIZE

Grips come in all shapes and sizes and it is essential to not only get the grip that feels the most comfortable, but also choose a grip that actually fits your hands correctly. A golf grip that is too small will often make the hands work too much during the swing, causing you to hook the ball; a grip too thick will stop the hands working and cause you to lose club head speed and distance. It can also change the flight of the ball dramatically and can even change the swing weight of the club, making the feel either too heavy or too light.

LOFT & LIES

LIE ANGLE

This is determined firstly by your height, but then more importantly by how shallow or steep the angle of attack you produce is when hitting the ball.

Getting this correct is quick and easy and, with a PGA pro watching you hit a few balls, should only take 10 minutes. Your pro will use a piece of equipment called a strike board. You hit a number of balls off the strike board, and a piece of tape placed on the sole of the club discolours as you do so, showing how the club sits when impacting the ball.

If the club is too flat, its toe will make contact with the ground first. As it does this, the clubface will open up causing you to push or even slice the ball. The same happens when the lie is too upright, and you will pull or even hook the ball. One degree out either way with a full seven iron shot can affect accuracy by up to 16 yards, and during a hole that could be the difference between making a birdie or running a big number and wrecking your scorecard.

CLUB LOFTS

Golf club lofts have changed very little over the years, and most of the equipment manufacturers work to the same, standard set of specifications. You will also see the average distances the clubs should fly and their trajectories.

The long irons have always been the more challenging clubs to hit, as they have the least amount of loft on them, so over the last 10 years many manufacturers have developed rescue clubs and hybrids to take their place. Many of the world's best golfers have dropped the 2 and 3-irons from their bags and now carry at least one hybrid and one rescue club. This enables them to hit the ball the same distance as before, but as the ball flies higher and lands softer it gives them much greater control. These clubs are great for the long par-threes and fours and, for the better golfers, the reachable par-fives.

TOP TIPS

It's possible to book days with manufacturers to try all of their products, but by visiting your PGA golf professional at your local club you will have access to a broader range of products and independent advice.

CHOOSING
THE STYLE OF IRON

There are now three styles of irons to choose from

BLADED IRONS

This style of club has been around since the dawn of time (as far as golf is concerned, anyway) and is the preferred choice for the single-figured golfer and pro. They are generally made from forged or form-forged soft steel and have a very small sweet spot, located in the middle of the clubface. They are very unforgiving and an off-centre hit can affect the distance the ball travels by up to 20 percent. Because the head-weight is spread more evenly higher up the clubface, the centre of gravity is raised, promoting a much lower ball flight. These clubs tend to have very little offset, which means that the leading edge of the club is more in line with hosel (where the club and shaft connect) making them less forgiving and causing you to hit the ground first, or promote a slice.

TOP TIP

Junior clubs also come in age sizes, and every PGA pro will be able to fit clubs for your child. Many of these can be extended as your child grows, making them a financially sound offer too. Nike, John Letters, Callaway and Wilson Staff will all custom fit your child.

HYBRID IRONS

These are the most forgiving and easiest clubs to use. They are a cross between a wood and an iron, with the bulk of the club's weight moved to the sole and extreme edges of the club. This makes the hybrid very effective for getting the ball airborne for a complete beginner or ageing golfer.

CAVITY-BACKED IRONS

These clubs started coming into circulation during the late 1970s, and are purely designed to make the game of golf easier. They do this by helping the golfer get the ball airborne, and are much more forgiving to off-centre hits than a bladed iron. What manufacturers found was that the more they moved the weight to the edges of the club, the larger the sweet spot became...and by moving some of that weight down to the sole of the club they were able to lower the centre of gravity. All this meant that, for the first time, even the worst golfers were able to start enjoying their rounds. Plus, the fact that the clubs were made from a cast and were cheaper to produce only enhanced the cavity-backed iron. Manufacturers were also able to move the leading edge of the club back, and found that this delayed the hitting of the ball by a fraction, making the clubface close slightly and reducing the amount of slice on the ball. The game's popularity exploded in the 1980s and, with new municipal or public golf courses being opened all around the country, golf was becoming both affordable and accessible.

GOLF TERMINOLOGY

A

Address: When you, the golfer, takes his stance, has lined up the club and are ready to swing.

Air shot: Completely missing the ball during your swing.

Albatross: Three shots under par.

Amateur: A golfer that doesn't play for prize money and doesn't make a profit from the game.

Approach: Hitting the ball in to the green.

B

Back nine: The last nine holes on the course.

Backspin: Striking the ball in a manner which sees is rotate backwards, landing to a stop more abruptly than usual.

Backswing: When you take the club away from you address position and continue until the club has reached the top of your swing.

Ball marker: A small disc-like object used to mark a ball's position on the green.

Birdie: One shot taken below par.

Bogey: One shot taken above par.

Break: The path that the ball takes across the slopes on the green.

Bunker: A hazard filled by sand or grass to make the golf course harder. You are not allowed to practice swing or ground your club in a bunker.

C

Casual water: Puddles on the course that are caused by heavy rain.

Chip: Hitting the ball close to the green so it lands on the surface and rolls to the hole.

Closed face: Turning the clubface slightly inward in order to hook the ball or prevent a slice.

Closed stance: Leading foot is nearer to the ball at address. Position normally adopted in order to hook the ball or prevent a slice.

Club head: The end of the club that includes the club face.

Club loft: The different angles of the clubface – these affect the flight and distance of the ball fly when the ball is hit.

D

Divot: A piece of turf torn when struck by a club.

Dogleg: A hole where the fairway bends to the left or right.

Double bogey: Two shots over par.

Downswing: The down part of the swing when hitting the ball.

Draw: Spin placed on the ball that makes the ball curl in flight.

Drive: A shot from the tee area.

Drop: Bringing the ball back into play after striking the last shot out of bounds or into a water hazard etc. The ball is released from an outstretched arm held at shoulder height.

E

Eagle: Two under par for a hole.

F

Fade: Spin placed on the ball that makes the ball curl gently in flight.

Fairway: The closely mown area between the tee and the green.

Fat shot: When the club strikes the ground well behind the ball.

Flex: The point at which the club shaft bends when swinging and hitting the ball.

Follow-through: That part of a golfer's swing after the ball has been struck.

Fore: "Fore" is shouted to warn other players that your ball is hit in their direction.

Forged: A club where the head is made from one piece of metal hammered into shape.

Four Ball: Where two pairs of golfers play in matchplay against each other.

Foursome: A group of four golfers playing only two balls. A pair of the players form a team and players alternate shots. The match can be scored as match play, stroke play or in Stapleford formats.

Front nine: The first nine holes.

G

Green fee: The cost to play the course.

Grip: The part of the club which the golfer holds.

Groove: The cut lines on the club face which create spin on the ball.

Gross score: Your score over 18 holes before you reduce it by taking your handicap away.

Grounding the club: To place the club on the ground prior to striking the ball when addressing it.

H

Halve a hole: In match play when you draw the hole.

Halve a match: In match play when you draw over 18 holes.

Handicap: The number of strokes a player is given to adjust his score after he has completed his round.

Handicap system: A method of adjusting golfers' scores to standard scratch so that they can compete on equal terms.

Hazard: Permanent features on the golf course designed to make the course more difficult to play.

Hole in one: When the ball goes straight into the hole from your tee shot.

Hole out: To get the ball into the hole.

Hook: To induce sidespin onto the ball causing in to move from outside to in on your swing. Opposite is slice.

I

Interlocking grip: To hold the club such that the little finger of one hand is wrapped around the forefinger of the other.
Iron: A metal headed club that is not a wood.

L

Lateral water hazard: A water hazard which runs parallel to the fairway.
Lie: The position of the ball at rest.
Line: The path of the golf ball.
Line of putt: The intended travel of the ball after it has been struck on the green.
Links: Golf course within four miles of the coast.
Local rules: Additional rules pertaining to a given course.
Loft: The angle of the clubface.
Loose impediments: Natural objects on the course, which are not fixed into place such as stones.

M

Match play: Form of competition where each hole is won, lost or halved. The winner is whoever wins the most holes.
Mulligan: When a player is allowed to retake a shot without penalty.
Municipal course: Golf course owned by local council and open to the public.

O

Open stance: At address the golfer stands with his front foot further from the ball line than his back foot.
Out of bounds: The area on the course where the ball may not be played from, marked by white posts.
Overlapping grip: To hold the club such that the little finger of one hand is wrapped around the forefinger of the other.

P

Penalty stroke: A stroke added to a player's score due to a rule infringement, taking relief from a hazard or an unplayable lie.
PGA: Professional Golfers Association.
Pin high: Means that the ball has landed on the green level with the hole as you are looking at it.
Pitch: When the ball is hit high into the air onto the green using a lofted club.
Pitch and run: To pitch the ball onto the green using a club which enables the ball to continue rolling on impact.
Pitch mark: The indentation left by a ball on the green after it has landed.
Playing through: To allow golfers in the game behind your game pass you while you stand to one side.
Plugged ball: A ball that when it lands remains in it's own pitch mark.
Preferred lie: You may lift, clean and replace your ball on the fairway within 6 inches of where it came to rest, not nearer the hole.
Pro shop: Shop at golf club where golf equipment and green fees should be paid.
Provisional ball: The playing of a second ball from the same place as the first because the player is unsure of what may have happened to the first ball (i.e. it may be lost).
Putt: Act of striking a golf ball on the green.
Putter: Club mainly used on green for striking the ball.
Putting green: The area of short grass surrounding the hole.

R

R & A: The Royal and Ancient Golf Club of St Andrews which oversees golf in Europe, Asia and the Commonwealth.
Relief: To lift and drop the ball without penalty in accordance with the rules.
Reverse overlap: A putting grip where the little finger of one hand is placed over the index finger of the other.
Rough: The high grass area adjacent to the fairway and green.

S

Sand wedge: An iron club designed to lift balls out of bunkers.
Shaft: That part of the club in steel and graphite between the head and the grip.
Short game: Chipping, pitching and putting.
Slice: To induce too much sidespin onto the ball causing it to travel through the air following inside to out swing. Opposite is hook.

Stableford: Point scoring competition. One point for a bogey, two points for a par, three for a birdie, four for an eagle and five for an albatross.
Stance: Where your feet are placed during your swing .
Standard scratch score: The score a scratch golfer should get when playing a course in normal conditions.
Stroke play: Where the winner of a match or competition is the player who used the least number of strokes (after handicap deduction) to complete the course.
Sweet spot: The preferred spot on the clubface with which to strike the ball.
Swing plane: The angle at which you swing the club round your body.

T

Takeaway: The first part of the golf swing.
Tee time: Scheduled start time.
Tempo: The speed of a golfer's swing.
Thin shot: When the clubhead strikes too high on the ball, causing low flight trajectory. Generally caused by players pulling their body up prior to impact or releasing the club too early on the downswing.
Top: To strike the ball above its centre causing it to skip and bounce along the ground rather than rise through the air.

W

Water hazard: Ponds, lakes, rivers or ditches on the course, always marked by yellow or red posts.
Winter green: A temporary green used in winter to protect the main greens.
Winter rules: Local rules which apply during the winter season only.
Wood: Clubs used for distance tee shots.

Y

Yardage chart: A printed card detailing the layout and yardage of each hole on the course.
Yips: To miss simple putts because of nerves.

GREAT GOLFING
UK SHORT BREAKS

★★★★★

THE K CLUB
GOLF & SPA RESORT

DUBLIN 2 NIGHTS, B&B, 2 ROUNDS FROM £175PP

The magnificent K Club has long enjoyed its position among the finest golf resorts in Ireland but, in late 2006, it was catapulted into the worldwide golfing spotlight when the Ryder Cup came to town. Since then golf fans from all over the world have come to learn that it is one of the finest golf break destinations in Europe.

With two stunning championship golf courses, five star luxury and a fantastic location just a short drive from Dublin, The K Club is a must for any golfer embarking on an Irish golf break. For those of you who enjoy a challenge, the Palmer Course has been tipped by many as the most difficult inland layout on the Emerald Isle.

★★★★★

CELTIC MANOR RESORT

SOUTH WALES

The famous Celtic Manor is at the forefront of the recent meteoric rise of Welsh golf. Following the success of the 38th Ryder Cup in 2010, golfers from across the world will be drawn to create their own golfing memories, following in the footsteps of the victorious European Team.

★★★★

THE VALE RESORT

SOUTH WALES

The Vale Resort is home to two championship golf courses, the much acclaimed 7,433 yard Wales National and the Lake – further boosting Wales' burgeoning reputation as an elite golfing destination.

★★★★

CARTON HOUSE HOTEL

DUBLIN

Carton House has emerged in recent years as one of the most exquisite golfing destinations in Ireland, as a result of two terrific, well-maintained courses, and an unrivalled level of service.

★★★★★
FOTA ISLAND RESORT & SPA

CORK

Fota Island is home to no less than three top-quality championship courses, and as such is one of the best golfing venues in Ireland. Set amidst the beautiful scenery of this corner of County Cork, the Sheraton Fota Island hotel is a real delight. All 131 bedrooms and suites are elegantly appointed, many of which allow superb views across the surrounding woodland and golf course.

★★★★
PORTMARNOCK HOTEL & LINKS

DUBLIN

Bernhard Langer was blessed with a remarkable piece of land on which to build what is now a classic links golf course. While it may be part of a golf resort, the layout is a genuine links, and with its proximity to Dublin, it is a fantastic place for a golf break.

★★★★
ST PIERRE
HOTEL & COUNTRY CLUB

CHEPSTOW

The two excellent golf courses at St Pierre - one of which is championship length at 7,028 yards - have been instrumental in the establishment of the resort as one of the best in Wales, well worth a trip.

★★★★★
LOUGH ERNE RESORT
COUNTY FERMANAGH

1 NIGHT, B&B, 2 ROUNDS
FROM £165PP

Lough Erne is the most exciting new golf destination in Ireland, endorsed by Rory McIlroy and set to establish itself as one of Europe's 'must play' destinations. The lakes of County Fermanagh set an unrivalled natural scene for a unique property, with golf, leisure and accommodation of the highest order.

★★★★
THE BELFRY
WARWICKSHIRE
1 NIGHT, DINNER, B&B, 2 ROUNDS
FROM £125PP

The Belfry is renowned as one of the world's most prestigious golfing destinations, having hosted the Ryder Cup on four occasions, but there is more on offer than just The Brabazon.

★★★★
OLD THORNS MANOR COUNTRY ESTATE

HAMPSHIRE

Old Thorns Manor Hotel, Golf & Country Estate is tucked away in 400 acres of rolling Hampshire countryside. It is one of southern England's most picturesque country-house-style hotels, and offers luxury accommodation, relaxing health spa facilities, fantastic cuisine and an outstanding 18-hole championship golf course, designed by the BBC's 'voice of golf' and the club president, Peter Alliss.

★★★★
ST MELLION RESORT

CORNWALL

Following a comprehensive £20 million redevelopment, the St Mellion International Resort now features the recently opened brand new 4* hotel plus significant improvements to the Nicklaus Signature Course and the Kernow Course (formerly the Old Course).

★★★★
MACDONALD LINDEN HALL

NORTHUMBERLAND

Linden Hall has a superb resort course, whose parkland layout will be enjoyed by all those who visit, whilst remaining a genuine challenge for even the best. Some excellent holes have been carved out by designer Jonathan Gaunt, who has used the indigenous landscape to create natural hazards.

★★★★★
STAPLEFORD PARK

LEICESTERSHIRE

1 NIGHT, DINNER, B&B, 2 ROUNDS
FROM £139PP

Stapleford Park's golf course is one of the most peaceful and tranquil to be found anywhere, being situated in the stunning Capability Brown gardens that surround the exquisite stately home. As the course winds around the house, it is never more than two holes wide, and the most threatening feature is the meandering River Eye, which comes into play on four occasions.

★★★★★
EAST SUSSEX NATIONAL

SUSSEX

East Sussex National boasts two championship courses that were designed by Robert E. Cupp, one of Jack Nicklaus' course architects, with major championship golf in mind. The resort has hosted two European Opens on the European Tour and played host to some of the world's leading players including Nick Faldo, Ernie Els, Vijay Singh, Colin Montgomerie, Jose Maria Olazabal, Nick Price and Ian Woosnam.

★★★★
BROCKET HALL

HERTFORDSHIRE

Brocket Hall, in the shadow of the majestic stately home, is among the most exclusive and desirable golf clubs anywhere in Britain. Boasting two championship golf courses, Michelin starred restaurant Auberge du Lac and the Palmerston Golf Academy, the facilities are outstanding, and are all set against the backdrop of the estate's majestic woodland and parkland.

★★★★
CROWNE PLAZA RESORT – FIVE LAKES

COLCHESTER, ESSEX

After a multimillion pound refurbishment during 2011 Five Lakes re-opened it's doors as Crowne Plaza Resort Colchester – Five Lakes, the first Crowne Plaza Resort Hotel in the UK. The resort features two superb golf courses, set in 320 acres of glorious Essex countryside, which has helped it to establish a reputation as one of the premier golfing destinations in the East of England.

★★★★

DALMAHOY, A MARRIOTT HOTEL & COUNTRY CLUB

EDINBURGH

Dalmahoy boasts two excellent golf courses and fantastic golfing facilities, making it one of the most complete golf destinations around the Lothians. Both the Solheim Cup and the Scottish PGA Championships have been held here in recent years, to demonstrate the quality on offer.

★★★★

MACDONALD CARDRONA

PEEBLES

Renowned course architect Dave Thomas' brief at Cardrona was to create a beautiful and challenging layout, completely harmonious with the extraordinary surrounding landscape. He has succeeded emphatically.

★★★★

MACDONALD MARINE & SPA

EAST LOTHIAN

The Macdonald Marine Hotel is gloriously situated, adjacent to the 16th green on the West Links at North Berwick's golf club. The imposing Victorian building has been restored to its former glory since its takeover by the established Macdonald chain, and its 83 rooms now ensure visitors a luxurious stay.

★★★★★

FAIRMONT ST ANDREWS

FIFE

1 NIGHT, B&B, 2 ROUNDS
FROM £130PP

Fairmont St Andrews boasts two tremendous links courses perched on the cliffs above St Andrews Bay, which have been widely recognised as a welcome addition to the world-famous courses at the St Andrews Links. Designed by Sam Torrance and Bruce Devlin, both courses are links in style, but have been built to suit the demands of a top-class resort. As such, they are playable for golfers of all standards, with a variety of tees from which to choose.

★★★★★
GLENEAGLES
PERTHSHIRE
1 NIGHT, B&B, 1 ROUND
FROM £175PP

The three wonderful courses at Gleneagles bear the hallmarks of two of golf's greatest names; five-time Open Championship winner James Braid laid out both the King's and Queen's courses, while all-time great Jack Nicklaus added the stunning PGA Centenary Course. Playing any of the three courses at Gleneagles is a delightful experience, with the springy moorland turf underfoot, the green hills to the South, and the peaks of the Trossachs and Ben Vorlich to the West.

CASTLE STUART GOLF LINKS
INVERNESS

Castle Stuart is the most exciting project to be undertaken in UK golf since Kingsbarns opened for play, and promises to transform the face of golf in the Scottish Highlands. Located just a few minutes from Inverness, the astounding golf course sits, precariously at times, on the banks of the Moray Firth.

★★★★
QHOTELS WESTERWOOD
NEAR GLASGOW

The golf course at the Westerwood was designed by Seve Ballesteros and Dave Thomas, and is one of the best golf courses to be opened in Scotland in recent years. A must try for golfers of all and every standard.

★★★★
CARNOUSTIE HOTEL & SPA
ANGUS

The Carnoustie Hotel is ideally situated adjacent to the first tee on the Championship Course, and directly behind the 18th green, affording magnificent views across the links towards the Angus coastline.

For details of breaks featured in this article visit **www.yourgolftravel.com**

GOLFING ABROAD

★★★★★
MOON PALACE

The Moon Palace sits on acres of lush, tropical shoreline and enjoys 2,000 ft of silky white sand beachfront. There are over 2,400 guest rooms and suites, 15 buffet and à la carte restaurants, swimming pools, tennis courts and two fitness centres to keep you entertained. The Moon Palace is home to two superb 18-hole Jack Nicklaus signature courses, and the Playacar course, about a 45-minute drive away, is an excellent Robert von Hagge design.

MEXICO

Golf in Mexico is booming, and with the variety, prices and extra-golfing activities on offer, it's not hard to see why. Mexico is one of the most beautiful, varied countries in the world and this is reflected in the country's superb golf courses. You'll find beach, jungle and urban courses all on offer – often designed by some of the biggest names in course design (think Nicklaus and Von Hagge) – meaning a new golfing experience waits round every corner.

★★★★★
SECRETS SILVERSANDS

Surrounded by warm crystal waters, this adults-only luxury resort features an expansive 43,000 sq ft. of pool areas complete with swim-out suites and manicured gardens. Designed for young souls, Secrets Silversands boasts an array of enticing amenities including exceptional gourmet dining, daily poolside activities and exciting nightlife. Complimentary green fees at nearby Grand Coral Riviera Maya Golf Club are also included, which features a magnificent 18-hole, 7,043 yard golf course designed by PGA champion Nick Price only steps away from the breathtaking Caribbean Sea.

★★★★★
DREAMS RIVIERA CANCUN

Surrounded by glistening pools, lush tropical gardens and a palm-studded beach, Dreams Riviera offers an array of amenities for every age and interest; from the Explorer's Club (a supervised kids club) to a variety of daily activities, nightly entertainment and gourmet à la carte dining. Your package also includes complimentary greens fees at nearby Gran Coral Golf Riviera Maya Golf Club, the same course mentioned left in the Secrets Silversands resort.

Fly Virgin Atlantic to
the home of Golf.

From April, Virgin Atlantic will begin
flying for the very first time between
Edinburgh and Aberdeen and London.

To book your next golfing holiday,
visit **www.destinationgolf.co.uk**

And don't forget.
Golf clubs travel free
as a matter of course.

virgin atlantic

★★★★★

ROVOS RAIL THE 2 SAFARIS

If you're after a golfing holiday with difference look no further than the spectacular Rovos Rail Golf Safari. Board this gorgeous train in South Africa's Pretoria and chug towards Cape Town, stopping at a broad variety of golf clubs and exciting tourist attractions along the way. On the golfing front these include rounds at the famous Leopard Creek Golf Estate and Durban Beachwood Country club, while attractions include taking part in a game drive at Kruger Park and a visit to the Ngwenya Glass Factory.

SOUTH AFRICA

South Africa has long been a favourite destination for golfers of all abilities. The country's broad mix of courses, from costal to high altitude, means there's something for everyone, and the beautiful African climate means time on the golf course is guaranteed...you can safely leave your waterproof suit and umbrella at home. If you needed any more encouragement, South Africa is home to the Gary Player Country club, an explosive course (generally considered the best in the country) located in an (extinct) volcano.

To book call: 01737-771613
or visit us online www.greatgolfdestinations.co.uk

virgin atlantic

DESTINATION
GOLF

Enjoy Upper Class from
pick up to takeoff.

Door-to-door limo at both
ends, and a jaw-to-floor
Clubhouse at the airport.

Find out more at
virginatlantic.com

upperclass

virgin atlantic

★★★★★
WESTIN MISSION HILLS

Two world-class golf courses and extensive recreational facilities allow guests to take full advantage of the ideal climate offered by California. This golfer's paradise is made up of two championship courses, the Gary Player Signature Course, which blends remarkably with the natural desert landscape, while the Pete Dye Course is one of the area's loveliest, but toughest, courses. The press have praised the remarkable Gary Player course as being "difficult, well-designed, and joyful" also stating that it "may be the best golf course in the Palm Springs area".

CALIFORNIA

Many have made the pilgrimage to one of golf's greatest locations, but if it's your first foray to The Golden State you've plenty to look forward to. The sheer variety on offer is stunning, and whether you're keen to mix it with the millionaires in Beverly Hills, or yearn for the searing heat of Palm Springs (with it's unique setting of rocky peaks and desert) there's plenty on offer. If you fancy a bit of time off the golf course, why not hit the Pacific for some surfing, or experience the fantastic skiing.

★★★★★
LA QUINTA

Come experience the grandest of Greater Palm Springs hotels, nestled at the base of the Santa Rosa Mountains. Unwind in exquisite Spanish-style casitas, suites and villas, revitalize body and mind at Spa La Quinta or spend the day lounging by one of 41 sparkling pools. La Quinta features five exceptional golf courses designed by the likes of Jack Nicklaus, Pete Dye and Greg Norman, so test your skills on the PGA West Tournament Course, the Mountain Course, Dunes Course, PGA West Stadium Course and PGA West Norman Course. All both unmissable and unforgettable.

★★★★★
PALM MOUNTAIN

This beautiful spa offers some of the finest holiday experiences in Palm Springs, and you'll love relaxing by the sparkling pool, or pampering yourself with a soothing massage. Enjoy the beautiful new guest accommodation, attentive staff and striking mountain views, lushly landscaped courtyards and spectacular swimming pool terrace. Golfers are also spoiled for choice, with Indian Canyons, Tahquitz Creek and the Escena Golf Club all within striking distance. The latter offering a critically acclaimed Jack Nicklaus designed course ideal for all standards.

To book call: 01737-771613
or visit us online www.greatgolfdestinations.co.uk

virgin atlantic   DESTINATION **GOLF**

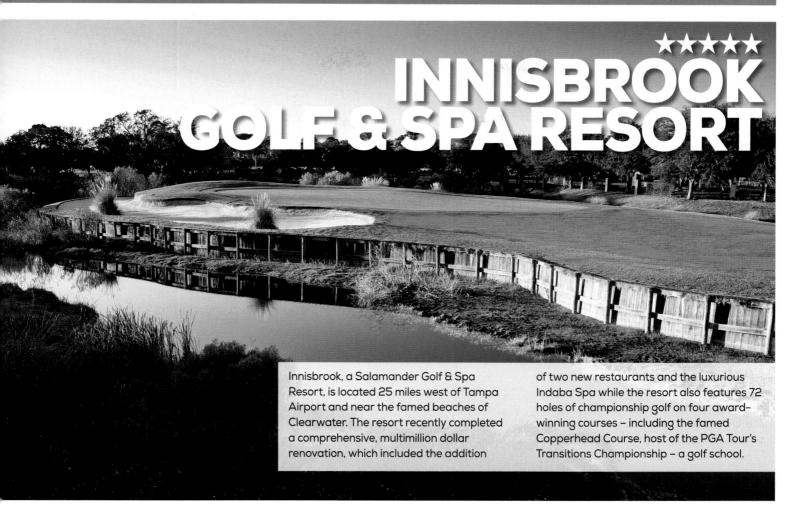

★★★★★
INNISBROOK GOLF & SPA RESORT

Innisbrook, a Salamander Golf & Spa Resort, is located 25 miles west of Tampa Airport and near the famed beaches of Clearwater. The resort recently completed a comprehensive, multimillion dollar renovation, which included the addition of two new restaurants and the luxurious Indaba Spa while the resort also features 72 holes of championship golf on four award-winning courses – including the famed Copperhead Course, host of the PGA Tour's Transitions Championship – a golf school.

★★★★★
NAPLES BEACH HOTEL

Located on the white sands of Naples, Florida, the Naples Beach Hotel is the only Florida beachfront resort with on-site golf, tennis, spa, and water recreation. With over $40 million spent in recent renovations, this newly remodelled resort features 317 rooms and suites, a new beachside pool complex, retail shopping, several restaurants/bars, complimentary Kids Klub and renovated greens and tees. With an 18-hole golf course on site (also recently renovated), this resort is the only Naples property that offers both a beachfront and on-site golf...and is not to be missed.

★★★★★
SADDLEBROOK

Saddlebrook is the proud home of one of Florida's friendliest golf resorts. The hotel itself boasts a wealth of top-draw rooms, amenities and services, meaning whether you're looking for a golf break or simply the chance to recharge your batteries, you'll find plenty to do. Saddlebrook offers two Arnold Palmer designed courses. Both have recently been renovated and offer excellent playing for all standards, so ideal for the whole family. There is also the excellent Saddlebrook Golf Academy for those looking to improve their game.

FLORIDA

It's fair to say that Florida, the Sunshine State, is golf mad...but it's not hard to see why. The state's climate makes year round golfing a real possibility, while over 1,000 public and private courses make it a sport available to everyone, regardless of budget. The courses are of the highest quality, too, and you'll find championship courses designed by the likes of Jack Nicklaus and Arnold Palmer (amongst many others) scattered between the Atlantic Ocean and Gulf of Mexico. A wealth of fantastic resorts and hotels also makes Florida one of the logistically easy golfing locations to stay at.

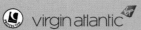

To book call: 01737-771613
or visit us online www.greatgolfdestinations.co.uk

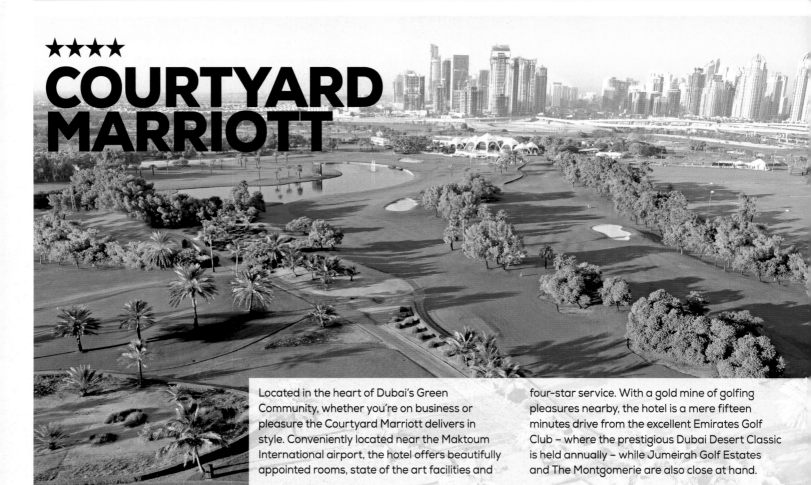

★★★★
COURTYARD MARRIOTT

Located in the heart of Dubai's Green Community, whether you're on business or pleasure the Courtyard Marriott delivers in style. Conveniently located near the Maktoum International airport, the hotel offers beautifully appointed rooms, state of the art facilities and four-star service. With a gold mine of golfing pleasures nearby, the hotel is a mere fifteen minutes drive from the excellent Emirates Golf Club – where the prestigious Dubai Desert Classic is held annually – while Jumeirah Golf Estates and The Montgomerie are also close at hand.

DUBAI

With its fantastic wealth and penchant for exciting engineering challenges, golf in the UAE has made massive strides in the last couple of decades. Nowhere is that more obvious than in Dubai, which features a number of first class golf courses. One of these is the famous Emirates Golf Club, which was not only the first grass golf club in the region nearly 22 years ago, but also hosts the prestigious Desert Classic, placing Dubai firmly on the golfing map.

To book call: 01737-771613
or visit us online www.greatgolfdestinations.co.uk

Swing your way to Scotland.

Virgin Atlantic's Flying Club is giving you the chance to test your drive against like-minded golfers in our Swingers Golf League. Climb the leader board by logging your scores and you could find yourself teeing off in our grand final in Scotland. Think you've got what it takes? Go to **flyingclubgolfleague.com** to register.

virgin atlantic

SUPPLIER
CONTACTS

APPAREL, WATERPROOFS & SHOES

Adidas	www.adidasgolf.com
Callaway	www.callawaygolf.com
Ecco	ecco.com/golf
FootJoy	www.footjoy.co.uk
Galvin Green	www.galvingreen.com
Glenmuir	www.glenmuir.com
IJP	www.ijpdesign.com
Kikkor	www.kikkor.co.uk
Mizuno	golf.mizunoeurope.com
Nike	www.nikegolf.eu
Oakley	http://uk.oakley.com
Ping	www.ping.com
ProQuip	www.proquipgolf.com
Stromberg	www.stromberggolf.com
Stuburt	www.stuburt.com
Sunderland	www.sunderlandgolf.com
Sunice	www.sunice.com
Tommy Hilfiger	www.tommy.com

Aquascutum	www.trendygolf.com
Hugo Boss	www.trendygolf.com
J. Lindeberg	www.trendygolf.com
Lyle & Scott	www.trendygolf.com
Puma	www.trendygolf.com
Ralph Lauren	www.trendygolf.com

RANGEFINDERS/TROLLEYS

Bushnell	www.bushnellgolf.com
Garmin	www.garmin.com/en-GB
GolfBuddy	www.golfbuddyglobal.com
Nikon	www.nikongolfrangefinders.com
SkyCaddie	www.skygolf.com

Hill Billy	www.hillbilly.co.uk
Motocaddy	www.motocaddy.com/uk
PowaKaddy	www.powakaddy.com
Stewart Golf	www.stewartgolf.co.uk/index.html

ACCESSORIES

Bollé	www.bolle-europe.co.uk
Golf Pride	www.golfpride.com
Oakley	uk.oakley.com
Serengeti	www.serengeti-eyewear.com
Swing Smart	www.swingsmart.co.uk
Taylor Made	http://taylormadegolf.eu
Trion:Z	www.trionz.co.uk

SUPPLIER CONTACTS

CLUBS, BALLS & GLOVES

Ben Sayers	www.bensayers.co.uk
Benross	www.benrossgolf.com
Bridgestone	www.bridgestonegolf.com
Callaway	www.callawaygolf.com
Cleveland	www.clevelandgolf.com
Cobra	www.cobragolf.co.uk
Dunlop	store.dunlopsport.com/golf
FootJoy	www.footjoy.co.uk
Honma	www.honmagolf.co.jp/en
Lynx	www.lynxgolf.co.uk
Mizuno	golf.mizunoeurope.com
Never Compromise	www.nevercompromise.com
Nike	www.nikegolf.eu
Odyssey	www.odysseygolf.com
Ping	www.ping.com
Srixon	www.srixon.co.uk
Taylor Made	http://taylormadegolf.eu
Titleist	www.titleist.co.uk
Wilson Staff	www.wilson.com/en-gb/golf

OAKLEY FAST JACKET XL
RRP: £190
http://uk.oakley.com

BOLLÉ BOLT
RRP: £120
www.bolle-europe.co.uk/.com

SERENGETI
RRP: £194
www.serengeti-europe.co.uk/.com

SWINGSMART
RRP: £199
www.swingsmart.co.uk

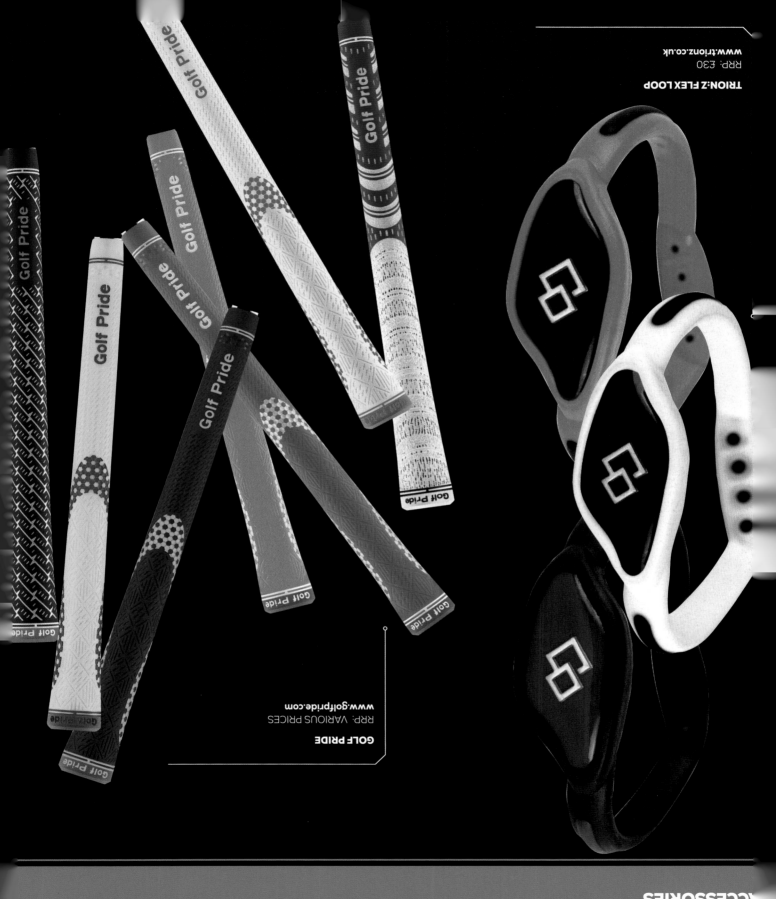

TRION:Z FLEX LOOP
RRP: £30
www.trionz.co.uk

GOLF PRIDE
RRP: VARIOUS PRICES
www.golfpride.com

TAYLOR MADE

LEFT | **RBZ STAGE 2** | RRP: £30
RIGHT | **DIVOT TOOL** | RRP: £10
http://taylormadegolf.eu

PREMIER PLUS GOLF ACCEORIES

ABOVE | **HEADCOVERS** | RRP: £15
RIGHT | **AQUA-LOCK TOWELS** | RRP: £15
www.premierplusgolf.co.uk

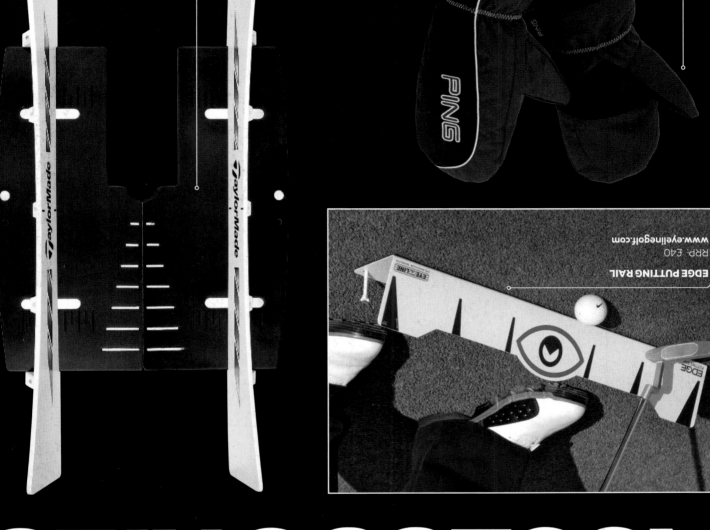

MUST HAVE
ACCESSORIES

STEWART GOLF

Stewart Golf is the Rolls-Royce of the motorised trolley market and the company's award-winning F1 model is powered by lithium batteries and controlled by a remote as standard. Meanwhile, the X7 model comes in four colours and boasts a 24-month warranty. It's also recognised as one of the finest remote controlled machines available. The new Z3 push trolley has received excellent reviews since launch. It's able to accommodate any size of golf bag, and if your bag doesn't fit, you will be offered a full refund.

STEWART GOLF

X7 LITHIUM REMOTE | RRP: £1,000
www.stewartgolf.co.uk

STEWART GOLF

F1 LITHIUM | RRP: £1,500
www.stewartgolf.co.uk

STEWART GOLF

Z3 PUSH TROLLEY | RRP: £180
www.stewartgolf.co.uk

HILL BILLY

These are incredibly light and easy-to-use electric trolleys. The Terrain, pictured left, is designed to be very robust and is powered by a 200W motor with speed control. It boasts a highly impressive 9kg weight (excluding the battery) making this a very compact and portable option.

HILL BILLY

TERRAIN | RRP: £270
www.hillbilly.co.uk

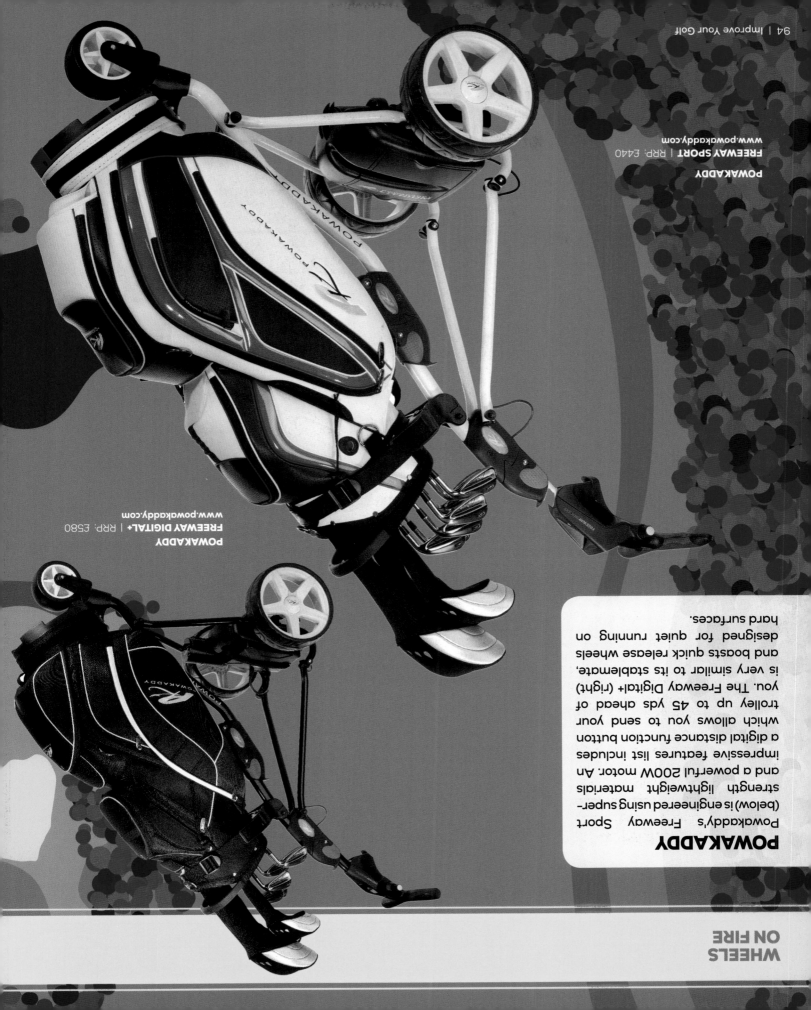

WHEELS
ON FIRE

POWAKADDY

Powakaddy's Freeway Sport (below) is engineered using super-strength lightweight materials and a powerful 200W motor. An impressive features list includes a digital distance function button which allows you to send your trolley up to 45 yds ahead of you. The Freeway Digital+ (right) is very similar to its stablemate, and boasts quick release wheels designed for quiet running on hard surfaces.

POWAKADDY
FREEWAY SPORT | RRP: £440
www.powakaddy.com

POWAKADDY
FREEWAY DIGITAL+ | RRP: £580
www.powakaddy.com

MOTOCADDY
M1 PRO | RRP: £400
www.motocaddy.com/uk

MOTOCADDY

Motocaddy's impressive range of electric golf trolleys is spearheaded by the company's M1 Pro compact folding model, seen here. It's one of the world's most feature packed trolleys, boasting distance measurement and control, a USB charging port, universal battery tray and nine speed settings. Its easy fold mechanism makes it one of the more easily stowed carts on the market.

WHEELS ON FIRE

G olf trolleys – push and electric – have been around for decades, but it's only in the last decade that the latter have become commonplace (and even more recently that they've become truly affordable). That doesn't make them cheap, but where golf buggies are a rarity the investment is well worth it. Not only will handy features like a digital scorecard make your life easier but, as our fitness section on page 100 of the tutorial section attests, saving you the physical effort of carrying your clubs can have a hugely positive impact on your fitness...and your game.

Never Compromise have four ranges of putters, the most expensive of which is the Gambler. The Sub 30 range featured opposite has a face insert manufactured from copper-infused aluminium and copolymer, which offers a soft feel and greater control of distance and direction. The taller face insert also minimises a loss of accuracy on off-centre hits. **Cleveland's** classic collection features the new face milled finish, which provides exceptional performance and a more responsive feel. **Benross'** putter range is light and bright, offering a splash of colour to your bag. They feature modern face grooves to promote topspin and roll. As with the Cleveland, milled-face technology gives you a little extra feel.

1. **Honma Beres BH-001** | RRP: £325 | www.honmagolf.co.jp/en
2. **Honma Beres PP-001** | RRP: £575 | www.honmagolf.co.jp/en
3. **Honma Beres PP-002** | RRP: £575 | www.honmagolf.co.jp/en
4. **Benross Casino Moi Shooter** | RRP: £80 | www.benrossgolf.com
5. **Benross Casino Anaconda** | RRP: £70 | www.benrossgolf.com

GALVIN GREEN ARLY - £269

Galvin Green's vibrant half-zip garment features Gore-Tex Paclite technology with stretch inserts to make this one of the most comfortable waterproof jackets going. Freedom of movement is second to none, and a host of features including water repellent zippers and adjustable neck, chest and cuffs make this an excellent choice.

SUNDERLAND RESORT CONVERTIBLE JACKET - £99

Sunderland are one of the biggest names in golfing apparel, and their waterproofs offer a combination of high quality and value for money. The jacket's soft laminated outer shell is 100% weatherproof, while the high collar protects your neck and back from rain, wind and snow. In warmer weather, you can even use the zips to convert the jacket to a half-sleeve...a useful feature.

FOOTJOY PERFORMANCE
LIGHT RAIN JACKET - £80

Despite looking and feeling like a windbreaker, Footjoy's 2013 Light Rain Jacket is actually fully weatherproof and extremely breathable. Sealed seams and a storm collar add extra functionality, while a scorecard pocket and two-year warranty make this an intelligent option for those ready to do battle with the elements.

NIKE STORM-FIT
GOLF JACKET - £99

This subtle, figure-hugging option from Nike will appeal to those after an understated jacket stuffed with technology. Cut from stretchable, seam-sealed material, the Storm-Fit jacket will ensure you stay warm and dry regardless of the conditions, allowing you to concentrate purely on your game. The material is also extremely pliable, leaving you complete freedom of movement.

MIZUNO PERFORMANCE SHELL RAIN JACKET – £99

An impressively tough option from Mizuno, the Performance Rain Shell is designed to keep you dry in even the most stormy of conditions. A three-layer construction featuring Mizuno's storm-busting 10,000mm Impermalite waterproofing system combines nicely with a five-year warranty.

PROQUIP TROPHY JACKET - £150

Proquip are the preferred suppliers of clothing to the 2014 Ryder Cup teams, so you can expect quality from the manufacturer. A laminated outer layer provides excellent yet sustained breathability and waterproofing in adverse weather conditions, while the materials used are tailored to be silent and flexible.

PING HYDRO WATER-PROOF GOLF JACKET - £80

This nicely understated jacket from Ping offers all the features a modern golfer needs to keep dry on the golf course. The light, breathable fabric is – like the Proquip jacket here – designed to be quiet, allowing you to concentrate on your game. It's also very competitively priced.

WATERPROOFS

SUNICE ELMONT - £250

This stylish number from Sunice (a company with ski-wear heritage) will certainly appeal to the younger generations and fashion conscious. Packed to the gills with the latest in wind and waterproofing Gore-Tex technology (including the excellent Paclite, ensuring it's light weight), this jacket is a must have for anyone looking to hit the courses this winter.

THE SHORT STUFF

PING NOME 500

RRP: £299
www.ping.com

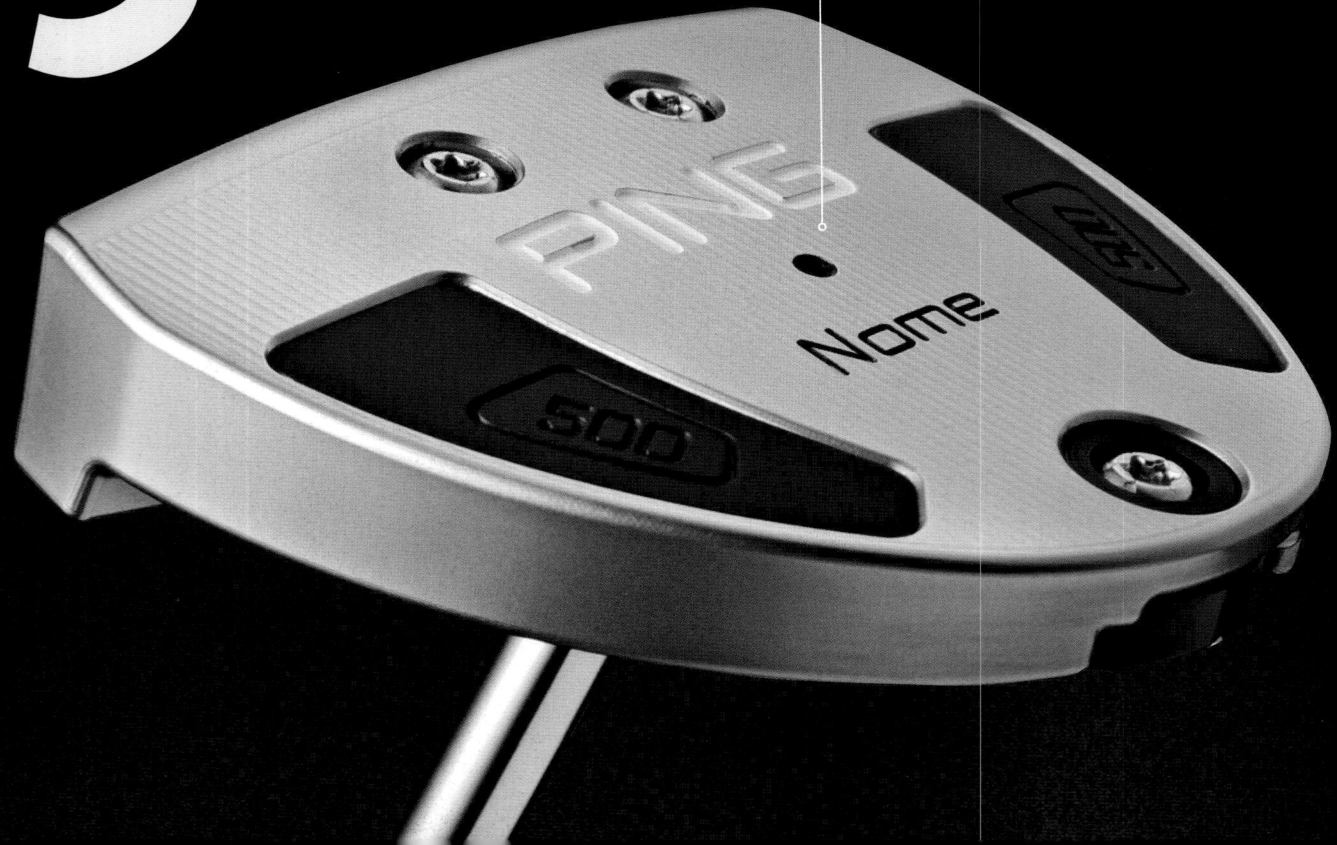

PING ANSER

RRP: £199
www.ping.com

DRIVE FOR SHOW, BUT PUTT FOR DOUGH... THIS YEAR'S PUTTERS WILL WIN YOU POINTS

The **Ping** Anser model has been around since 1959 and very little has changed in its design in the intervening years. It's the classic heel toe weighted putter and comes in a broad variety of styles and finishes. Ping's mallet style Nome putter features a lightweight aluminium frame with a tungsten sole weighting. It optimises the centre of gravity with the aim of giving better feel and roll. The Scottsdale Hohum putter is available in face-balanced and heel toe weighted models. The Scottsdale range of putters includes the Anser 2 and Mesquite models, and each has thermo elastomer inserts which give exceptional feel and distance control.

PING SCOTTSDALE HOHUM

RRP: £125
www.ping.com

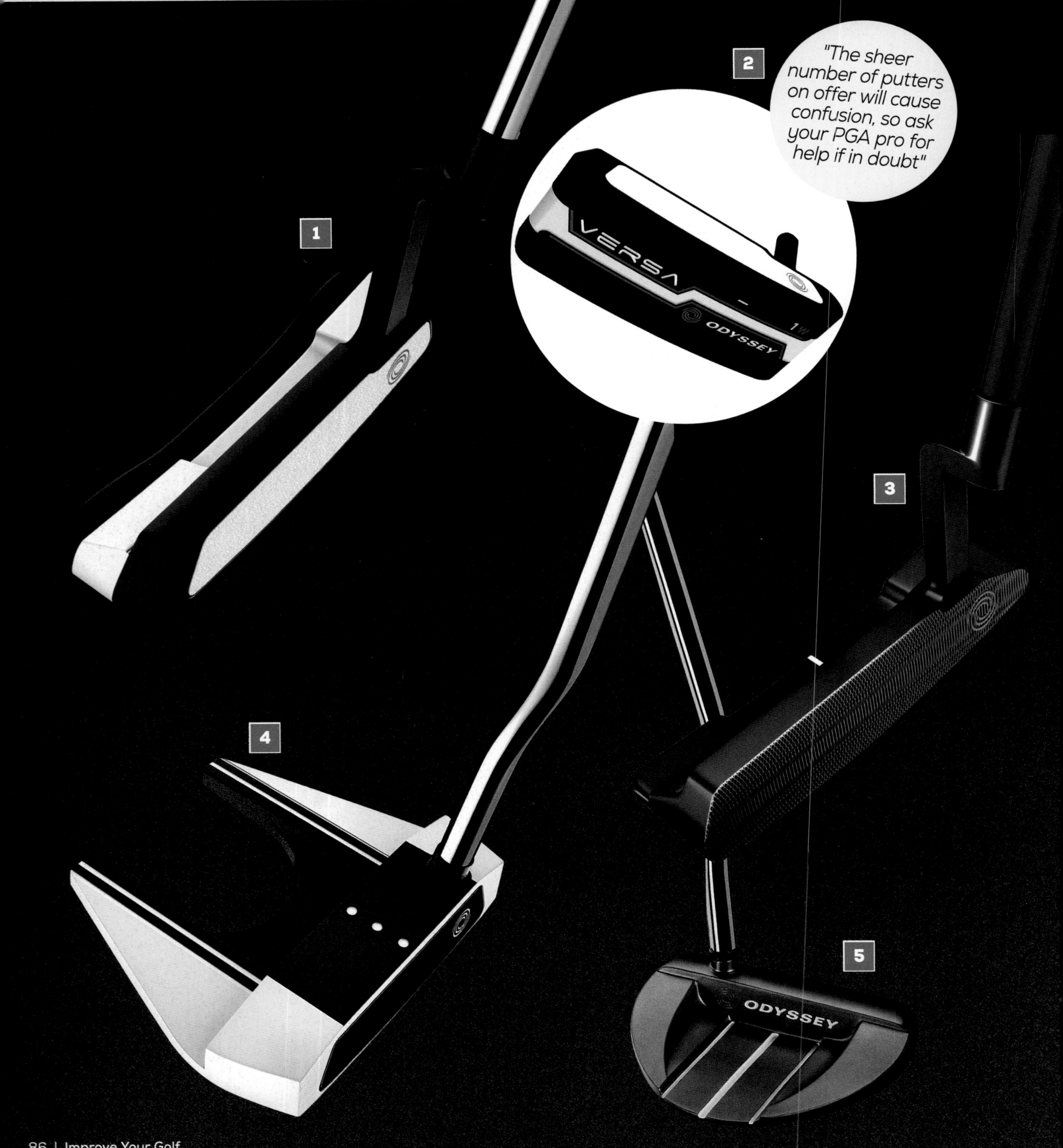

1

2

"The sheer number of putters on offer will cause confusion, so ask your PGA pro for help if in doubt"

VERSA

ODYSSEY 1W

3

4

5

ODYSSEY

6

7

ESSENTIAL PUTTING TIPS

- Greens are slower in the wet, be direct
- Don't over think a putt – go for it
- The reverse overlap grip is the most used
- One smooth consistent stroke is crucial
- Take into account the wind when putting

The 2013 Callaway **Odyssey** putter range has a huge variety of products to offer the golfer, and you'll find 11 models to choose from, each with a number of variations. The Versa putter, expected to be a big seller for Odyssey in 2013, features a number of black and white colour combinations, allowing you to choose the colour scheme that feels most comfortable for you. Elsewhere all other styles of putter can be found, from the classic blade putter of the 1920s to the mallet headed models of more modern times.

8

ODYSSEY PUTTERS

1. **Versa #1** | RRP: £119 | **www.odysseygolf.com**
2. **Versa #1 Wide Putter** | RRP: £119 | **www.odysseygolf.com**
3. **ProType Black #2** | RRP: £209 | **www.odysseygolf.com**
4. **Versa #7** | RRP: £119 | **www.odysseygolf.com**
5. **White Hot Pro V-Line** | RRP: £109 | **www.odysseygolf.com**
6. **ProType Black 2-Ball** | RRP: £229 | **www.odysseygolf.com**
7. **Versa #9** | RRP: £119 | **www.odysseygolf.com**
8. **White Hot Pro D.A.R.T. Mini** | RRP: £150 | **www.odysseygolf.com**

SELECT BIG SUR LONG

RRP: £278
www.titleist.co.uk

SELECT NEWPORT 2

RRP: £225
www.titleist.co.uk

CALIFORNIA MONTEREY

RRP: £278
www.titleist.co.uk

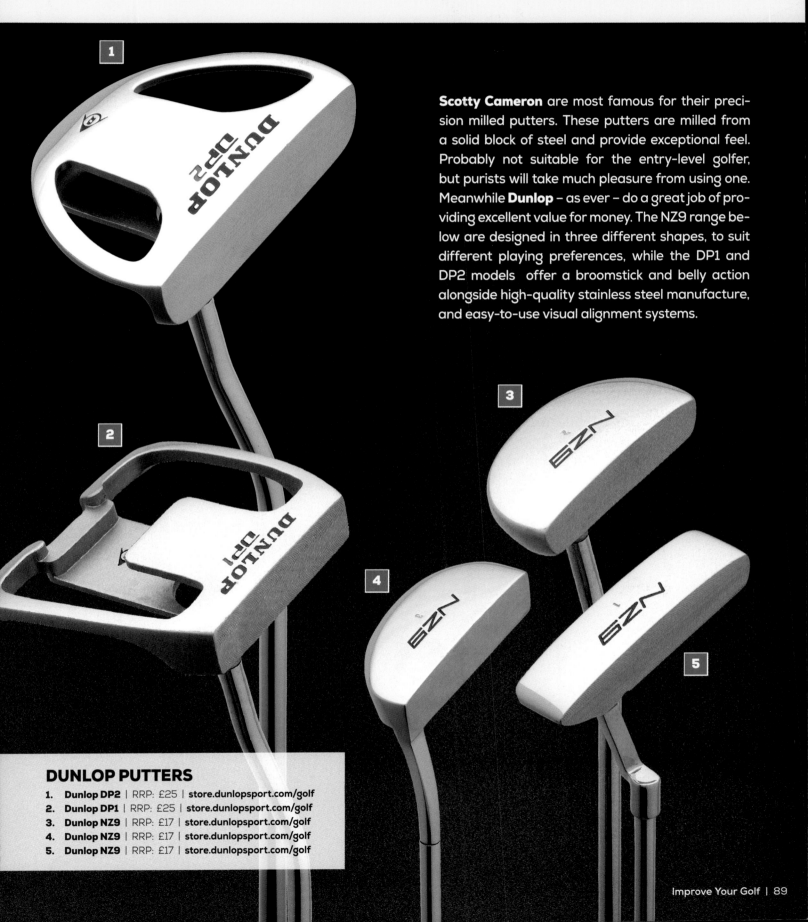

Scotty Cameron are most famous for their precision milled putters. These putters are milled from a solid block of steel and provide exceptional feel. Probably not suitable for the entry-level golfer, but purists will take much pleasure from using one. Meanwhile **Dunlop** – as ever – do a great job of providing excellent value for money. The NZ9 range below are designed in three different shapes, to suit different playing preferences, while the DP1 and DP2 models offer a broomstick and belly action alongside high-quality stainless steel manufacture, and easy-to-use visual alignment systems.

DUNLOP PUTTERS

1. **Dunlop DP2** | RRP: £25 | store.dunlopsport.com/golf
2. **Dunlop DP1** | RRP: £25 | store.dunlopsport.com/golf
3. **Dunlop NZ9** | RRP: £17 | store.dunlopsport.com/golf
4. **Dunlop NZ9** | RRP: £17 | store.dunlopsport.com/golf
5. **Dunlop NZ9** | RRP: £17 | store.dunlopsport.com/golf

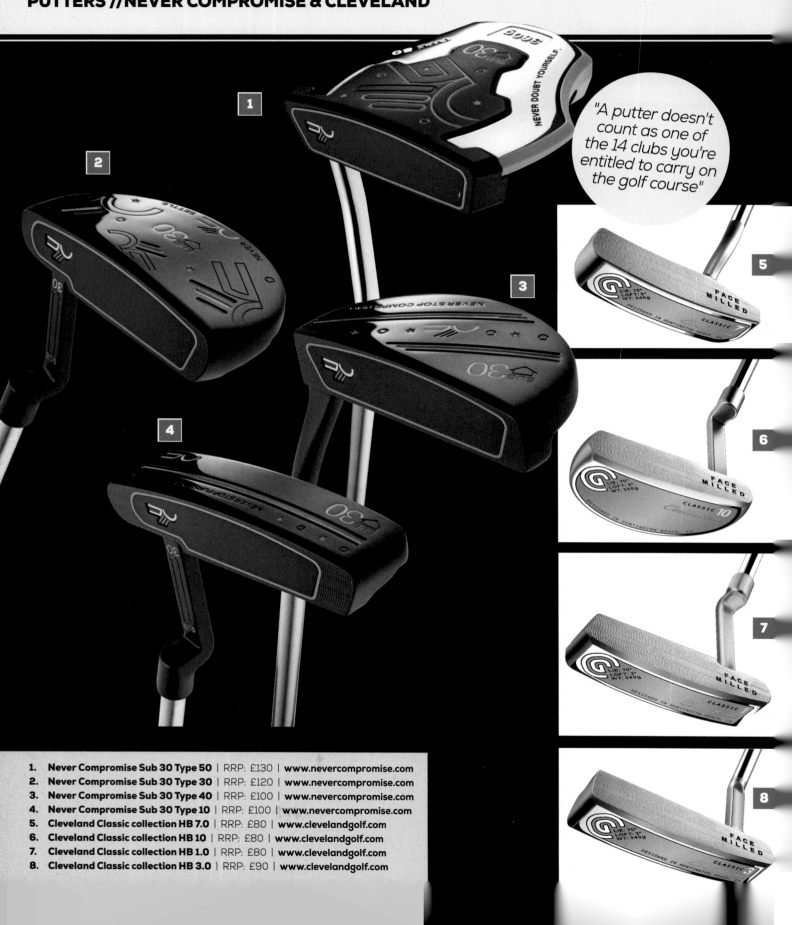

"A putter doesn't count as one of the 14 clubs you're entitled to carry on the golf course"

1. **Never Compromise Sub 30 Type 50** | RRP: £130 | www.nevercompromise.com
2. **Never Compromise Sub 30 Type 30** | RRP: £120 | www.nevercompromise.com
3. **Never Compromise Sub 30 Type 40** | RRP: £100 | www.nevercompromise.com
4. **Never Compromise Sub 30 Type 10** | RRP: £100 | www.nevercompromise.com
5. **Cleveland Classic collection HB 7.0** | RRP: £80 | www.clevelandgolf.com
6. **Cleveland Classic collection HB 10** | RRP: £80 | www.clevelandgolf.com
7. **Cleveland Classic collection HB 1.0** | RRP: £80 | www.clevelandgolf.com
8. **Cleveland Classic collection HB 3.0** | RRP: £90 | www.clevelandgolf.com

STORM CHASER

Getting soaked is one of the primary reasons a golfer will abandon a round. That's a shame, because there are a plethora of fantastic waterproof options to keep you on the golf course in adverse weather conditions. It's also important to remember that if you're playing a competition, you might not have the option to abandon ship, so let's take a look at this year's best waterproof wear.

STUBURT

TOP | Darren Clarke Collection | RRP: £150
BOTTOM | Helium FSZ | RRP: £70
www.stuburt.com

PUMA

TOP | Fass Grip | RRP: £40
BOTTOM | AMP Cell Fusion SL | RRP: £80
www.puma.com

Most golf shoes have now moved away from the old spike system, literally a small metal stud, to a more course friendly soft spike. These soft spikes come in two kinds, the first of which can be seen on the **Mizuno's** below, while in the last five years many of the golf companies have now introduced dimpled-soled shoes that provide extra comfort on harder ground. Whichever spikes you prefer, it's always worth checking ahead to confirm if the golf club has a soft spike policy.

MIZUNO GENEM ELITE

RRP: £159
http://golf.mizunoeurope.com

OAKLEY CARBONPRO

RRP: £165

http://uk.oakley.com

NIKE LUNAR CONTROL

RRP: £120

www.nikegolf.eu

CALLAWAY XTREME

£120
www.callawaygolf.com

ADIDAS ADIZERO TOUR

RRP: £130
www.adidasgolf.com

Up until a few years ago the vast majority of golf shoes were constructed from leather (including the soles). Today, many manufactuers (including **Nike** and **Puma** here) have opted for lightweight synthetic materials that provide comfort, support and durability. These include new soles designed to provide as much grip as possible during the swing. Unlike leather shoes, you don't need to break in shoes manufactured from synthetic materials – and they won't break you in either.

FOOTJOY ICON

RRP: £200
www.footjoy.co.uk

KIKKOR

TOP | Player Tips | RRP: £80
BOTTOM | Slyder | RRP: £50
www.kikkor.co.uk

HI-TEC

TOP | V-Lite Splash | RRP: £35
BOTTOM | CDT Power | RRP: £60
www.hi-tec.com

ECCO

TOP | Biom Hybrid | RRP: £160
BOTTOM | Tour Hybrid | RRP: £160
ecco.com/golf

GOLF SPIKES

Golf shoes have evolved greatly over the last 10 years. Soles designed to increase your stability, balance and grip are combined with the latest technology and materials to produce lighter, stronger and more weather proof shoes.

With shoes ranging from £30 to £100 plus, the variety on offer is baffling, so we've compiled a list of 2013's top shoes to keep an eye out for.

TOP TIP:

ALWAYS REPAIR YOUR PITCH MARKS

THEY CAN TAKE UP TO THREE WEEKS TO FULLY RECOVER...

NIKE VR PRO FORGED WEDGE

RRP: £100
www.nikegolf.eu

"The bounce of a wedge plays a major role in determining how it performs in different conditions"

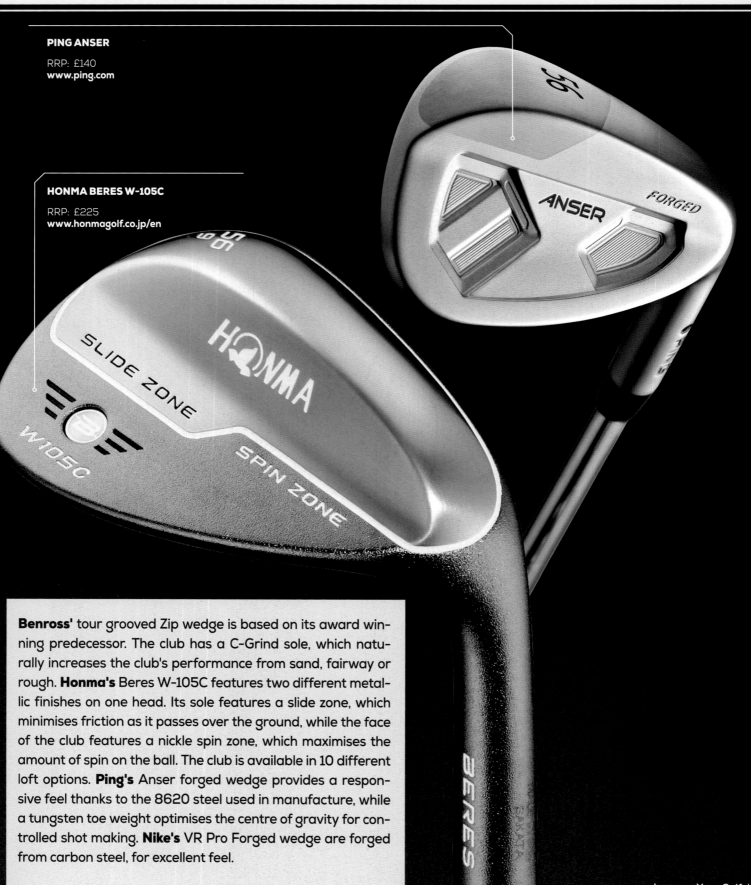

PING ANSER

RRP: £140
www.ping.com

HONMA BERES W-105C

RRP: £225
www.honmagolf.co.jp/en

Benross' tour grooved Zip wedge is based on its award winning predecessor. The club has a C-Grind sole, which naturally increases the club's performance from sand, fairway or rough. **Honma's** Beres W-105C features two different metallic finishes on one head. Its sole features a slide zone, which minimises friction as it passes over the ground, while the face of the club features a nickle spin zone, which maximises the amount of spin on the ball. The club is available in 10 different loft options. **Ping's** Anser forged wedge provides a responsive feel thanks to the 8620 steel used in manufacture, while a tungsten toe weight optimises the centre of gravity for controlled shot making. **Nike's** VR Pro Forged wedge are forged from carbon steel, for excellent feel.

MIZUNO MP-T4

RRP: £100
golf.mizunoeurope.com

"The most common fault in poor wedge play is excessive wrist action"

BENROSS

TOP | ZIP IT BLACK PEARL | RRP: £59
BOTTOM | ZIP IT COBALT | RRP: £69
www.benross.com

5

6

7

52

WEDGES

1. **Bridgestone J40** | RRP: £89 | www.bridgestonegolf.com
2. **Dunlop NZ9** | RRP: £18 | store.dunlopsport.com/golf
3. **Dunlop DP1** | RRP: £19.99 | store.dunlopsport.com/golf
4. **Callaway Forged Wedge** | RRP: £99 | www.callawaygolf.com
5. **Taylor Made RocketBladez** | RRP: £69 | http://taylormadegolf.eu
6. **Taylor Made ATV** | RRP: £80 | http://taylormadegolf.eu
7. **Titleist Vockey SM4** | RRP: £102 | www.titleist.com

"When deciding on using a wedge, always remember that they are for accuracy, not distance"

Bridgestone's J40 come finished in both black oxide and chrome, and the classic head shape was designed in conjunction with their tour staff, so any purchaser can enjoy the same clubs as the pros. As with all the manufacturers each comes in various lofts and bounces, so finding the perfect club shouldn't be a problem once you've spent some time trying them. **Taylor Made's** exciting ATV stands for All Terrain Versatility. Using it, you can play from bunkers, deep rough, flop shots and pitch shots with ease, making it a highly versatile club. The company's new RocketBladez wedge has a redesigned cavity to promote feel, and also features the above ATV technology. Bob **Vockey** remains the leading designer of sand wedges in the world. Since 1999 Vockey has designed wedges for 21 major champions, and each club is testament to his skill – a real artisan's club for the better play. This **Mizuno** MPT4 features quad cut grooves for better spin and is manufactured using Mizuno's grain flow forging technique, which provides enhanced feedback through the club head.

CLEVELAND WEDGES

1. **588 Forged RTG** | RRP: £119 | **www.clevelandgolf.com**
2. **588 RTX CB Black Pearl** | RRP: £109 | **www.clevelandgolf.com**
3. **588 Forged Satin** | RRP: £119 | **www.clevelandgolf.com**
4. **588 Forged Black Pearl** | RRP: £119 | **www.clevelandgolf.com**

SAND WEDGE

70% OF THE GAME IS PLAYED WITHIN 70 YARDS OF THE HOLE, ENSURE YOU'VE GOT THE BEST EQUIPMENT

Cleveland's 2013 range of 588 wedges come in many styles, options and finishes. From the traditional bladed sand irons through to the new satin and black pearl cavity backed wedges, there's something on offer for all styles and abilities of play. **Dunlop's** DP1 offers an excellent entry-level wedge, but for real value consider the NZ9, which features a tour-standard True Temper Dynamic gold shaft and anti-glare black finish. A 22-groove milled face should provide a great striking surface. **Callaway's** beautifully forged wedges (opposite) are an absolute must-try for any golfing connoisseur. These are classically designed, and a good example of a manufacturer at the top of it's game.

Tommy Hilfiger (above right)

TOP | PRESTON V-NECK | RRP: £65
SHIRT | LEON POLO | RRP: £55
SHORTS | BRISTOL BERMUDA SHORTS | RRP: £80
www.tommy.com

Puma

TOP | 1/4 ZIP STRIPE SWEATER | RRP: £69
SHIRT | COLOURBLOCK STRIPE | RRP: £49
TROUSERS | TECH PANT | RRP: £59
www.trendygolf.com

Ping (far right)

TOP | HENDERSON SWEATER | RRP: £50
SHIRT | DESI POLO | RRP: £50
TROUSERS | VOLT TROUSERS | RRP: £50
www.ping.com

TRENDYGOLF

TRENDYGOLF.COM

ON COURSE TO LOOK GOOD

Hugo Boss (right)

SHIRT | PADDY PRO 5 | RRP: £109
TROUSERS | HASSLY PRO 1 | RRP: £159
www.trendygolf.com

J Lindeberg (middle)

SHIRT | ADAM PRINTED FIELDSENSOR | RRP: £89
TROUSERS | NAVY PINSTRIPE NICOLAS | RRP: £112
www.trendygolf.com

Glenmuir (bottom)

SHIRT | PERFORMANCE FIT CLUB COOLMAX | RRP: £41
TROUSERS | BRANWELL COTTON STRETCH | RRP: £53
www.glenmuir.com

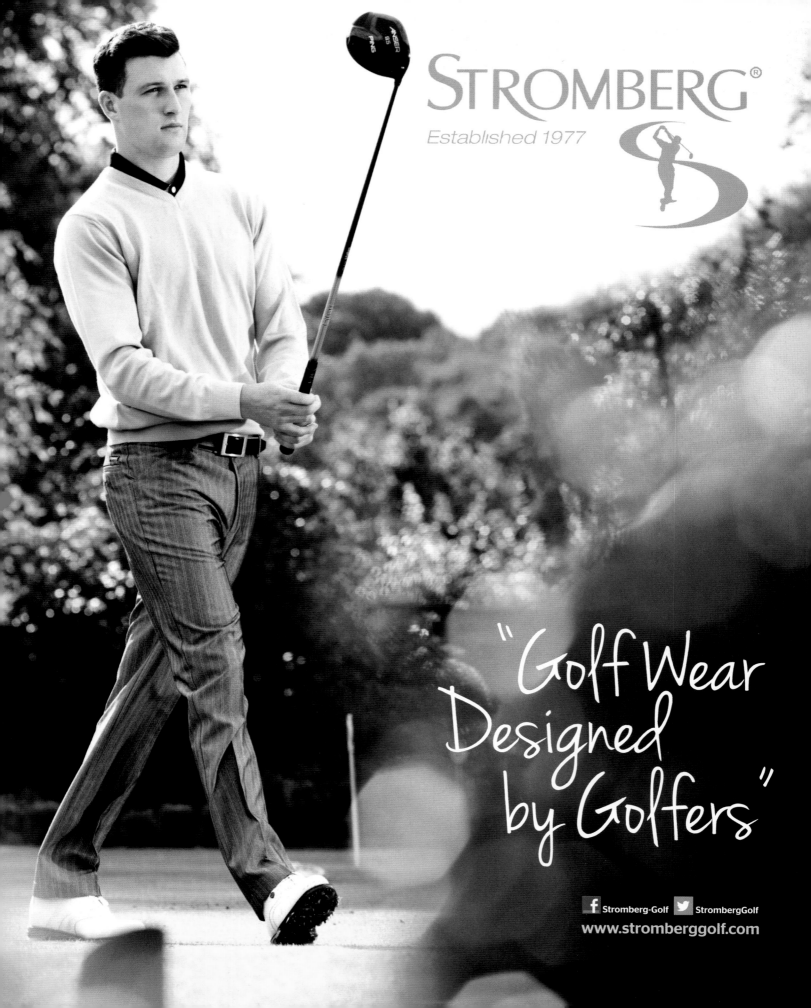

Galvin Green

SHIRT | MELVIN SHORT SLEEVE | RRP: £69
TROUSERS | NED VENTIL8 | RRP: £99
www.galvingreen.com

Oakley

TOP | OFF CENTRE 1/4 | RRP: £65
TROUSERS | CROSS TOWN PANTS | RRP: £55
http://uk.oakley.com

Polo Golf (right)

TOP | V-NECK SWEATER | RRP: £110
SHIRT | PRO FIT POLO | RRP: £69
TROUSERS | BARROW FIT PANT | RRP: £99
www.trendygolf.com

Nike (below)

SHIRT | ULTRA STRIPE POLO | RRP: £35
TROUSERS | MODERN TECH PANT | RRP: £55
www.nikegolf.eu

IJP

TOP | CREST V-NECK | RRP: £55
SHIRT | NEW VEGAS POLO | RRP: £65
TROUSERS | POULTER TARTAN | RRP: £100
www.ijpdesign.com

ON COURSE TO LOOK GOOD

The golf clothing industry has come a long way since the days of chinos and pique shirts. The apparel market is now a multimillion-pound industry that produces fashion-led garments crafted from the latest technical fabrics, offering trousers, shirts and jumpers (such as UV protection and moisture wicking) yesteryear's golfer could only have dreamed of.

Over the following pages we have put a few outfits together from all the big hitters, ensuring you look your best when you tee off at the first.

Aquascutum

TOP | 1/4 ZIP ARGYLE NAVY | RRP: £165
TROUSERS | TECHNICAL PANT | RRP: £149
www.trendygolf.com

Lyle & Scott (right)

TOP | HALF ZIP PULLOVER | RRP: £79
SHIRT | COLOURBLOCK POLO | RRP: £59
TROUSERS | TECHNICAL STRETCH TROUSER | RRP: £85
www.trendygolf.com

Stromberg (bottom)

TOP | RIVIERA/10 | RRP: £40
SHIRT | SAN ROQUE | RRP: £40
TROUSERS | SINATRA/3 | RRP: £40
www.stromberggolf.com

"A cavity backed iron is ideal for those after a little more forgivness"

Continuing their impressive run of recent form, **Bridgestone's** J40 forged cavity back iron (aimed at providing great feel and feedback) and the new J40 dual pocket cavity iron (designed for more forgiveness) are going to be hard to choose between. **Nike's** new VR_S Covert iron, again with a cavity back design, purports to give longer, straighter shots, while **Callaway's** X range family, with an extra deep cavity for a lower centre of gravity, has something for everybody. Since 1997 **Ben Ross'** CEO John Everitt has been producing outstanding quality products at affordable prices. The Speed range offers quality and affordability for golfers of all ability, making this a manufacturer you should seriously consider. **Honma** offer beautifully crafted clubs for the deep pocketed. The Japanese brand's Tour World irons are the big news for 2013, and a five star graphite set will cost you £26,995. **Lynx's** rebirth (three years in) continues apace and the brand always marries quality with affordability, while in 2013 **Ben Sayers** offer great value courtesy of this M11 complete set.

IRONS

"As the Honma Tour World range demonstrates, the lighter the material the club is made from, the pricier it is"

IRON MAN

1. **Bridgestone J40 Cavity Back** | RRP: £600 | www.bridgestonegolf.com
2. **Bridgestone J40 Dual pocket cavity** | RRP: £530 | www.bridgestonegolf.com
3. **Callaway X Forged** | RRP: £799 | www.callawaygolf.com
4. **Callaway X Hot** | RRP: £599 | www.callawaygolf.com
5. **Callaway X Hot Pro** | RRP: £699 | www.callawaygolf.com
6. **Cobra Amp Cell** | RRP: £549 | www.cobragolf.co.uk
7. **Nike VR_S Covert** | RRP: £449 | www.nikegolf.eu

8. **Benross Rip Speed Tour** | RRP: £380 | www.benrossgolf.com
9. **Benross Max Speed** | RRP: £200 | www.benrossgolf.com
10. **Benross Hot Speed** | RRP: £330 | www.benrossgolf.com
11. **Honma Beres IS-02** | RRP: £2,195 | www.honmagolf.co.jp/en
12. **Honma Tour World 717P** | RRP: £1,275 | www.honmagolf.co.jp/en
13. **Honma Tour World 717V** | RRP: £1,275 | www.honmagolf.co.jp/en
14. **Lynx Black Cat Plus** | RRP: £329 | www.lynxgolf.co.uk
15. **Ben Sayers M11 (comes as part of a set)** | RRP: £250 | www.bensayers.co

IRON MAN

Dunlop manufactures excellent entry-level equipment but, with the NZ9 iron aimed at the better player, now offer a high quality club at a very affordable price. **Ping**, meanwhile, never fails to impress and the manufacturer's new i20 and G25 range of stainless steel game improvement clubs look excellent options. The updated Anser soft forged steel irons (for the better player) round out what certainly appears to be an impressive 2013 range. A great looking **Wilson** range provides everything from the forged blade FG62 iron and soft carbon steel FG Tour V2, to the sleek Ci11. The thinner faced D-100 irons are a must-try for those after a little help with their shot making. 2013 sees **Taylor Made** introduce its RocketBladez iron in a tour and game improvement model, both designed to radically increase ball speed and distance.

"The clubhead features a hosel, which is the part where the shaft is connected"

IRON MAN

1. **Dunlop NZ9** | RRP: £280 | store.dunlopsport.com/golf
2. **Ping Anser** | RRP: £19.99 | www.ping.com
3. **Ping G25** | RRP: £620 | www.ping.com
4. **Ping i20** | RRP: £720 | www.ping.com
5. **Wilson Staff Ci11** | RRP: £389 | www.wilson.com/en-gb/golf
6. **Wilson Staff FG Tour V2** | RRP: £549 | www.wilson.com/en-gb/golf
7. **Wilson Staff D-100** | RRP: £349 | www.wilson.com/en-gb/golf
8. **Wilson Staff FG 62** | RRP: £599 | www.wilson.com/en-gb/golf

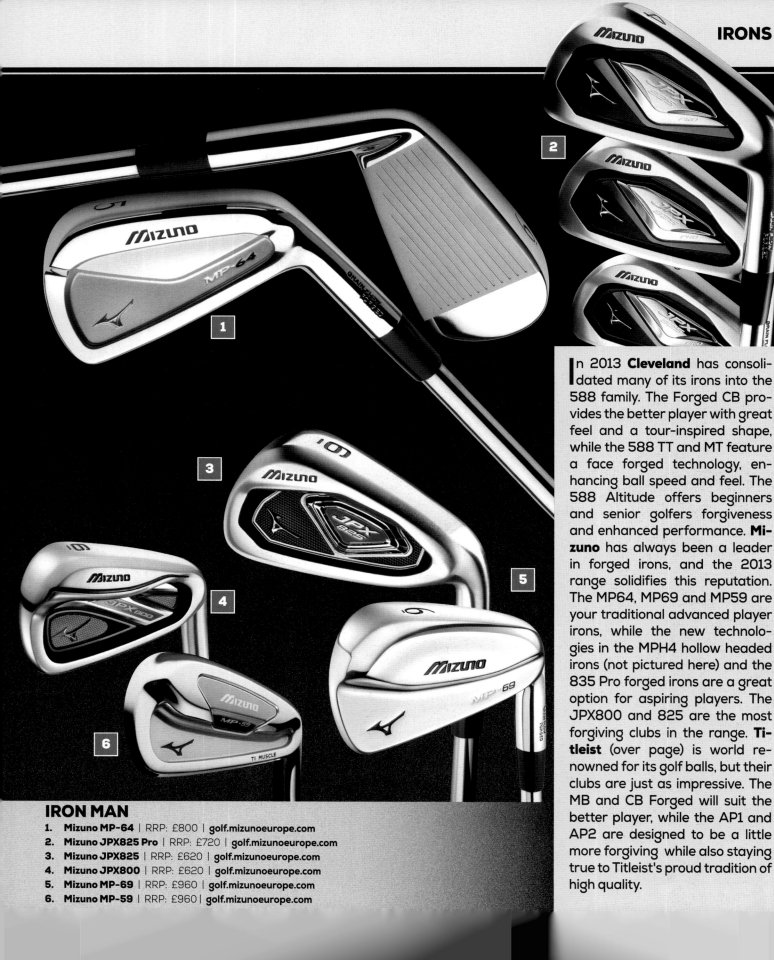

In 2013 **Cleveland** has consolidated many of its irons into the 588 family. The Forged CB provides the better player with great feel and a tour-inspired shape, while the 588 TT and MT feature a face forged technology, enhancing ball speed and feel. The 588 Altitude offers beginners and senior golfers forgiveness and enhanced performance. **Mizuno** has always been a leader in forged irons, and the 2013 range solidifies this reputation. The MP64, MP69 and MP59 are your traditional advanced player irons, while the new technologies in the MPH4 hollow headed irons (not pictured here) and the 835 Pro forged irons are a great option for aspiring players. The JPX800 and 825 are the most forgiving clubs in the range. **Titleist** (over page) is world renowned for its golf balls, but their clubs are just as impressive. The MB and CB Forged will suit the better player, while the AP1 and AP2 are designed to be a little more forgiving while also staying true to Titleist's proud tradition of high quality.

IRON MAN

1. **Mizuno MP-64** | RRP: £800 | **golf.mizunoeurope.com**
2. **Mizuno JPX825 Pro** | RRP: £720 | **golf.mizunoeurope.com**
3. **Mizuno JPX825** | RRP: £620 | **golf.mizunoeurope.com**
4. **Mizuno JPX800** | RRP: £620 | **golf.mizunoeurope.com**
5. **Mizuno MP-69** | RRP: £960 | **golf.mizunoeurope.com**
6. **Mizuno MP-59** | RRP: £960 | **golf.mizunoeurope.com**

IRON MAN

THE MEAT OF ANY CLUB SET, ALL PRICES HERE ARE FOR THE SET

CLEVELAND 588 ALTITUDE

RRP: £449
www.clevelandgolf.com

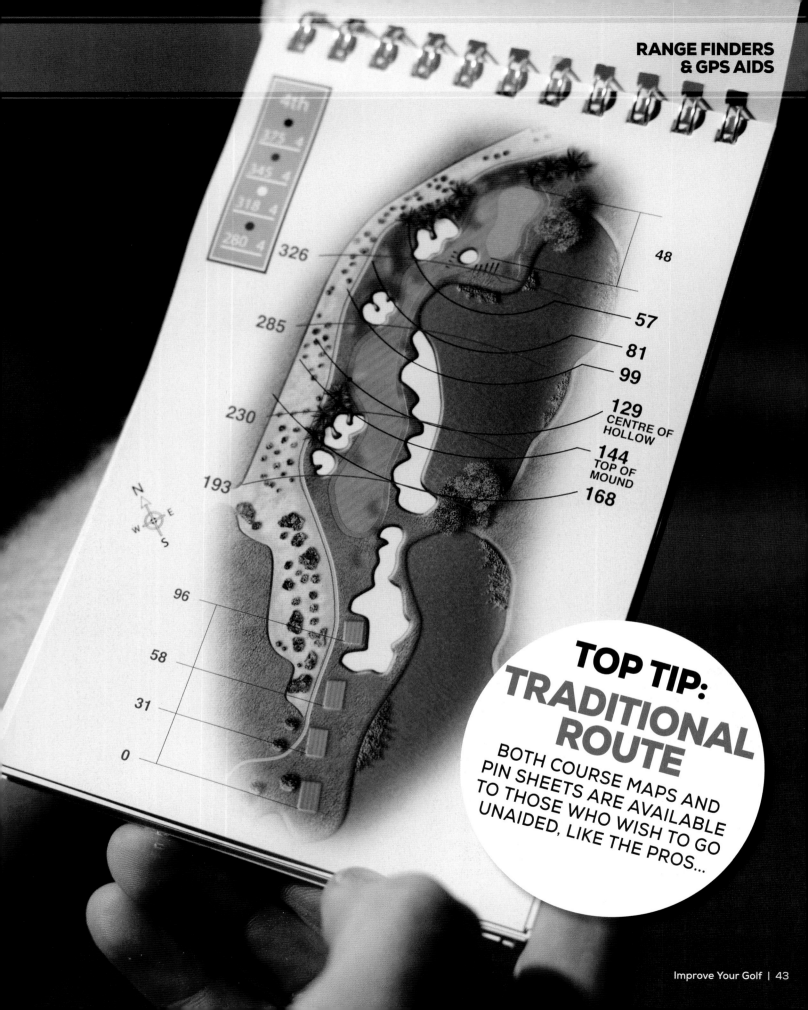

4th

326

285

230

193

48

57

81

99

129
CENTRE OF
HOLLOW

144
TOP OF
MOUND

168

N
E
W
S

96

58

31

0

TOP TIP: TRADITIONAL ROUTE

BOTH COURSE MAPS AND PIN SHEETS ARE AVAILABLE TO THOSE WHO WISH TO GO UNAIDED, LIKE THE PROS...

SkyCaddie

SkyCaddie is one of the biggest names in the golf GPS business, and is famed for cramming only the newest technology into their products. The Breeze is a fine example of this, and it acts as a virtual sprinkler head, giving you front, middle and back of the green distances from all angles. 30,000 courses come pre-loaded, although you do need a subscription for the full service, but the inbuilt shot measurer allows you to measure how far you're hitting each club, enhancing your knowledge of your own game and improving your golf. The range topping SGX features a omni-directional, high-performance anntenae, and is stuffed with the latest software advances. Interactive HoleVue gives you a flyby look at the pin from your approach shot for improved strategy, while IntelliGreen shows you the exact run of the green from whicever angle you approach it from, helping you avoid those 3-putts.

SkyCaddie Breeze | RRP: £230 | www.skycaddie.co.uk
SkyCaddie SGX | RRP: £270 | www.skcaddie.co.uk

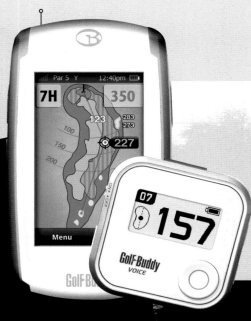

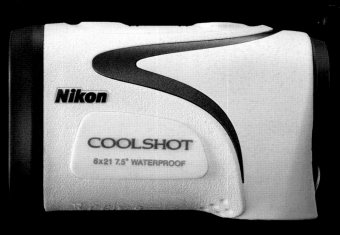

GolfBuddy

Golf Buddy has – as a company – over 40,000 courses mapped, making their devices one of the most comprehensive around. New to their 2013 range, the GolfBuddy Voice gives you audio distance information at the touch of a button, while its diminutive size lets you handily attach it anywhere, from the peak of a cap to your watch. The new Platinum GPS rangefinder features a high contrast LCD touchscreen for easy viewing in all lights. A statistics analysis module and digital scorecard help manage your round, while shock and waterproof casing prepare the Platinum for the rough and tumble of the golf course.

GolfBuddy Platinum | RRP: £330 | **www.golfbuddyglobal.com**
GolfBuddy Voice | RRP: £160 | **www.golfbuddyglobal.com**
Garmin Approach G6 | RRP: £330 | **www.garmin.com/en-GB**
Nikon COOLSHOT | RRP: £270 | **www.nikongolfrangefinders.com**

Garmin

The Approach G6 from Garmin features an astonishing 30,000 courses preloaded, and features a glove friendly, highly colourful touch screen. A digital scorecard is included and a 'club average' feature let's you constantly update how far you're hitting each club.

Nikon

Nikon's new compact COOLSHOT laser rangefinder is accurate to within half a yard from 600 yds and features a design that's ergonomically attractive and easy to use. It has a large ocular for simplified viewing and is waterproof. Distances are displayed in increments of 0.5 yds, making your game highly accurate, and it also gives you eight seconds of continuous measurement, enabling even the shakiest hands to get an accurate reading.

Bushnell

Bushnell's Z6 laser rangefinder is accurate to within an impressive half yard from 450 yds, and with 6x magnification makes targeting the flag easy. Rubber armoured metal housing makes the rangefinder extremely rugged, and a two-year warranty rounds off an attractive package. The Pro 1M is accurate to within one yard from an impressive 500yds. It has a visual display technology for all light conditions, features 7x magnification and is waterproof. The Neo+ GPS watch features 25,000 courses preloaded (with no subscription required) and has a very simple front, centre and back distances to the green feature.

TOP | **Tour Z6** | RRP: £349
MIDDLE | **Neo+ GPS Watch** | RRP: £159
BOTTOM | **Pro 1M** | RRP: £399
www.bushnellgolf.com

DEMAND PRECISION

Bushnell
GOLF

Lee Westwood

Introducing the Tour™ Z6 with Vivid Display Technology, by Bushnell®

TOUR Z6

ViVID DISPLAY TECHNOLOGY

PINSEEKER TECHNOLOGY INSIDE

"This new product is a testament to Bushnell and demonstrates yet again why they dominate the game. Their new technology, features and aesthetics make the Tour Z6 a pleasure to use whilst delivering yardage faster and more accurately than ever before. No other distance technology comes close."

Lee Westwood

THE #1 LASER RANGEFINDER — Bushnell — ON TOUR

THE N°1 LASER RANGEFINDER IN PROFESSIONAL GOLF *

www.bushnellgolf.co.uk   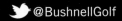 @BushnellGolf

OFFICIAL PARTNER

The National Golf Club Challenge

SUPPORTING HELP FOR HEROES

RANGE FINDERS & GPS AIDS:
FOR WHEN ACCURACY MATTERS...

Rangefinders are used across the world by golfers as a means of aiding them with their course management (see page 77 of the tutorials). There are two dominating technologies used: the laser rangefinder and the GPS rangefinder.

Laser rangefinders have been around since the 1990s, and were used by course mappers and tour professionals to gain accurate distances to help with club selection. Very simply the device fires a laser out at the target you're aiming it at. When the signal comes back the rangefinder will work out the distance for you.

GPS rangefinders are much more complicated. They're not as accurate as the laser rangefinders, but they instantly give you a bird's-eye view of the hole you're playing, providing information on where the trouble is and how far each feature of the hole is. They work using GPS satellite, the same technology used in car GPS navigation devices, and are now accurate up to about five yards. A must for serious golfers.

"a customisable loft option gives you greater trajectory control than ever before"

GET OUT OF JAIL...

1. **Ben Sayers M11 Hybrid (comes as part of a set)** | RRP: £250 | www.bensayers.co.uk
2. **Bridgestone J40** | RRP: £159 | www.bridgestonegolf.com
3. **Nike VR_S Covert** | RRP: £129 | www.nikegolf.eu
4. **Nike VR_S Covert Tour** | RRP: £159 | www.nikegolf.eu
5. **Titleist 913H** | RRP: £197 | www.titleist.co.uk
6. **Taylor made RocketBallz Stage 2 Tour Rescue** | RRP: £149 | http://taylormadegolf.eu

1

"Many will find great value in package sets, such as the Ben Sayer's M11 option featured here"

GET OUT OF JAIL...

1. **Ping G25** | RRP: £170 | www.ping.com
2. **Ping i20** | RRP: £160 | www.ping.com
3. **Ping Anser** | RRP: £180 | www.ping.com
4. **Callaway X Hot Hybrid** | RRP: £149 | www.callawaygolf.com
5. **Cleveland Classic Hybrid** | RRP: £129 | www.clevelandgolf.com

6. **Mizuno JPX825** | RRP: £129 | golf.mizunoeurope.com
7. **Honma Tour World TW717** | RRP: £495 | www.honmagolf.co.jp/en
8. **Honma Beres U-01** | RRP: starts at £525 | www.honmagolf.co.jp/en
9. **Honma 55th Anniversary Hybrid (part of a set)** | RRP: £12,450 | www.honmagolf.co.jp/en

player with a clean, square leading edge, making this utility highly workable. For those with cash to burn, the Honma 55th Anniversary club set is well worth a look. **Ben Sayer's** M11 utility club comes with the company's starter set package and is a great club for the beginner. **Bridgestone's** large headed utility, the J40, maximises its low profile design to produce a high launch angle, maximising its carrying distance. **Nike's** VR_S Covert hybrid has the new speed cavity back for longer, straighter shots, while the Tour hybrid has patented flex loft technology, enabling you to adjust the face angle and lofts for maximum shot making. The **Titleist** 913H features SureFit hosel technology which allows you to adjust the club's loft and lie yourself and to also adjust the clubs weight to your own specification. **Taylor Made's** RocketBallz Tour Rescue boasts exceptional ball spin, and sports the Taylor Made loft sleeve. This offers seven standard and five upright loft options that can add or subtract up to one-and-a-half degrees of loft.

GET OUT OF JAIL...

1. **Benross Hot Speed** | RRP: £90 | www.benrossgolf.com
2. **Benross Max Speed** | RRP: £90 | www.benrossgolf.com
3. **Benross Rip Speed** | RRP: £90 | www.benrossgolf.com
4. **Dunlop DP1** | RRP: £45 | store.dunlopsport.com/golf
5. **Dunlop NZ9** | RRP: £35 | store.dunlopsport.com/golf

TOP TIP:
IDENTIFY YOUR BALL

IT'S A TWO-SHOT PENALTY IF YOU PLAY THE WRONG BALL, SO MARK YOURS TO ENSURE YOU CAN IDENTIFY IT

MIZUNO MP650

RRP: £159
www.mizuno.com

COBRA AMP CELL HYBRID

RRP: £159
www.cobragolf.co.uk

GET OF OUT JAIL...

...FREE. AVOID THE TROUBLESOME 1, 2 AND 3-IRONS WITH THESE EASY HITTERS

Mizuno's MP650 is carried on the European Tour van, is used by Mizuno's tour players and is best suited to the better player. The JPX825 (on page 35) is a more forgiving hybrid that provides a higher trajectory and straighter shots. The Amp Cell hybrid from **Cobra** has all the latest technologies, including six adjustable settings that allow you to alter the club's loft, maximising distance and trajectory. The clubs also come in variety of attractive colours. **Benross'** Speed family of hybrids has something to offer every standard of player. The Rip Speed provides tour lofts and a sleeker profile, whereas the Hot and Max will suit the intermediate and beginner respectively. **Dunlop** hybrids are priced very competitively. The NZ9 is a great option for any standard of player, while the DP1 Hybrid is designed to provide higher, softer ball flights for the advanced golfer. **Ping's** G25 is designed for players af-

ter a higher trajectory ball flight and, while the Anser does have much in common with the G25, ultimately offers a slightly lower ball flight. The i20 gives the better player the option of an even lower ball flight. All feature a distinctive matte black finish, which reduces glare. The X Hot from **Callaway** comes with a Warbird Sole, making the club easier to use from any lie, while the Speed Frame face provides higher ball speed to maximise distance. **Cleveland's** Classic Hybrid comes with a gliderail sole, which decreases drag and provides more lift out of even the heaviest rough. Cleveland has also managed to optimise the club head's centre of gravity to maximise a higher launch with a more penetrating ball flight. **Honma's** U-01 utility comes with a nickel heel and toe weighting system, which enlarges the club's sweet spot, also producing a higher trajectory ball flight. The TW717 provides the better

GET A GRIP

Golf gloves have been worn since the 1930s, with Jack Nicklaus and Arnold Palmer early adopters. They provide the golfer with extra comfort when holding the club, and extra grip in adverse weather conditions. They are traditionally made using Pittards leather but in recent years – with the development of new fabrics and technologies – synthetic models (as sported by the Mizuno opposite) have started to appear. These provide both superb grip in the rain and thermal protection in the extreme cold.

1

PICK YOUR GLOVE

1. **Titleist Players Glove** | RRP: £17 | www.titleist.co.uk
2. **FootJoy StaSof** | RRP: £18 | www.footjoy.co.uk
3. **Nike Dri-FIT Tech** | RRP: £20 | www.nikegolf.eu
4. **Ping M-FIT** | RRP: £14 | www.ping.com
5. **Taylor Made TP** | RRP: £18 | http://taylormadegolf.eu
6. **Mizuno BIOFLEX** | RRP: £7 | golf.mizunoeurope.com
7. **Callaway X Hot All Weather** | RRP: £10 | www.callawaygolf.com

Cleveland's 2013 Classic XL fairways have one of the biggest faces on the market, making the club's sweet spot larger and more forgiving, suiting all abilities. **Lynx's** Black Cat fairway is a highly impressive club that features a low centre of gravity, offering a higher trajectory and great value. **Ping's** new Anser 3-wood offers trajectory tuning technology, allowing you to add or subtract half a degree of loft to the standard settings. The G25 has the thinnest face of any Ping fairway wood, creating faster ball speed, while the i20 offers a more compact head, making hitting out of heavy grass easy. **Dunlop's** feature full DP1 uses directional grooves to reduce drag in the swing, and makes a great choice for beginner golfers.

"If you're after greater ball penetration, try a fairway that produces less spin"

1

15.5°

2

"Most clubs come in a variety of different specifications and colours, so try before you buy"

3

POWER AND CONTROL

1. **Cleveland Classic XL** | RRP: £159 | www.clevelandgolf.com
2. **New Lynx Black Cat** | RRP: £99 | www.lynxgolf.co.uk
3. **Mizuno MP-650** | RRP: £189 | golf.mizunoeurope.com
4. **Dunlop DP1** | RRP: £45 | store.dunlopsport.com/golf
5. **Ping G25** | RRP: £199 | www.ping.com
6. **Ping i20** | RRP: £200 | www.ping.com
7. **Ping Anser** | RRP: £220 | www.ping.com

"The thinner the club's head, the faster ball speed you will get off it"

Callaway's 2013 X Hot family share a lot of technologies. Both feature a Forged Speed Frame Face Cup technology that increases ball speed across the club face, and an Internal Standing Wave (a groove in the sole) to reduce the centre of gravity. The RZR FIT XTREME is an excellent addition to the range, and features OptiFit tecnology, allowing extra control over the club's face angle. **Wilson's** D-100 fairway is one of the lightest clubs on the market, which helps you optimise your club head speed and distance while **Mizuno's** JPX825 features a large footprint and a ground hugging design. It's meant to enable you to hit the ball higher and straighter, and is suited to golfers of all standards.

Titleist's range of 913 fairway woods come with a classic pear shaped design. The company's F.d fairway (pictured left) provides a lower spinning option to give more penetrative ball flight, while clubs offer a SureFit tour hosel, which allows you to adjust your loft and lies. **Honma's** S02 3-wood is an excellent option for golfers looking for a higher trajectory flight, as the shaft provided has a low kick point offering greater lif. Homna's Tour World 3-wood (not pictured here) is designed to off better penetration for the advancded player. **Nike's** range of fairways boast a host of new technologies for 2013. The tour model (pictured below) offers FlexLoft technology, allowing you to later your loft and face angle on the fly.

"Grooves in a club's sole reduce drag – aiding speed – and lower the head's centre of gravity"

POWER AND CONTROL

1. **Titleist 913F.d Low Spin** | RRP: £215 | www.titleist.co.uk
2. **Titleist 913F** | RRP: £215 | www.titleist.co.uk
3. **Honma Beres S-02** | RRP: £525 | www.honmagolf.co.jp/en
4. **Nike VR_S Covert Tour** | RRP: £189 | www.nikegolf.eu
5. **Callaway RAZR FIT XTREME** | RRP: £199 | www.callawaygolf.com
6. **Callaway X Hot** | RRP: £179 | www.callawaygolf.com
7. **Honma Tour World TW717** | RRP: £495 | www.honmagolf.co.jp/en
8. **Mizuno JPX825** | RRP: £189 | golf.mizunoeurope.com
9. **Wilson Staff D-100** | RRP: £129 | www.wilson.com/en-gb/golf

TAYLOR MADE ROCKETBALLS STAGE 2

RRP: £189
http://taylormadegolf.eu

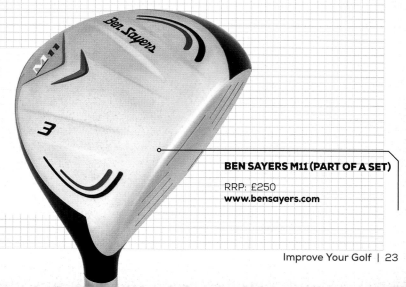

AWAY WITH THE FAIRWAYS

THIS YEAR'S BIG HITTERS PROVIDE POWER AND CONTROL

As with the company's drivers, **Taylor Made's** 2013 range of fairway woods features RocketBallz technology. This increases club head speed and promotes more distance, and is targeted at both intermediate golfers and tour golfers. A highly impressive range of clubs. As with the other **Ben Sayers** clubs featured in this equipment guide, the M11 fairway comes as part of a fantastic package that boasts both great value for money and high quality. Ideal for the starter golfer.

BEN SAYERS M11 (PART OF A SET)

RRP: £250
www.bensayers.com

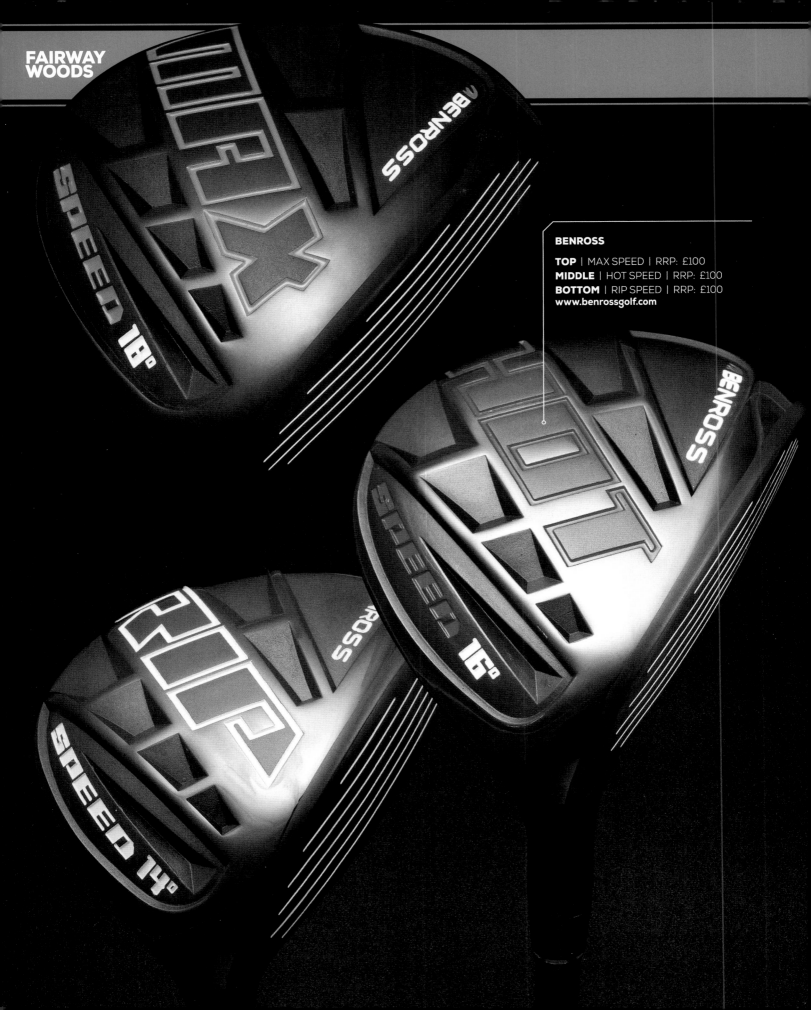

BENROSS

TOP | MAX SPEED | RRP: £100
MIDDLE | HOT SPEED | RRP: £100
BOTTOM | RIP SPEED | RRP: £100
www.benrossgolf.com

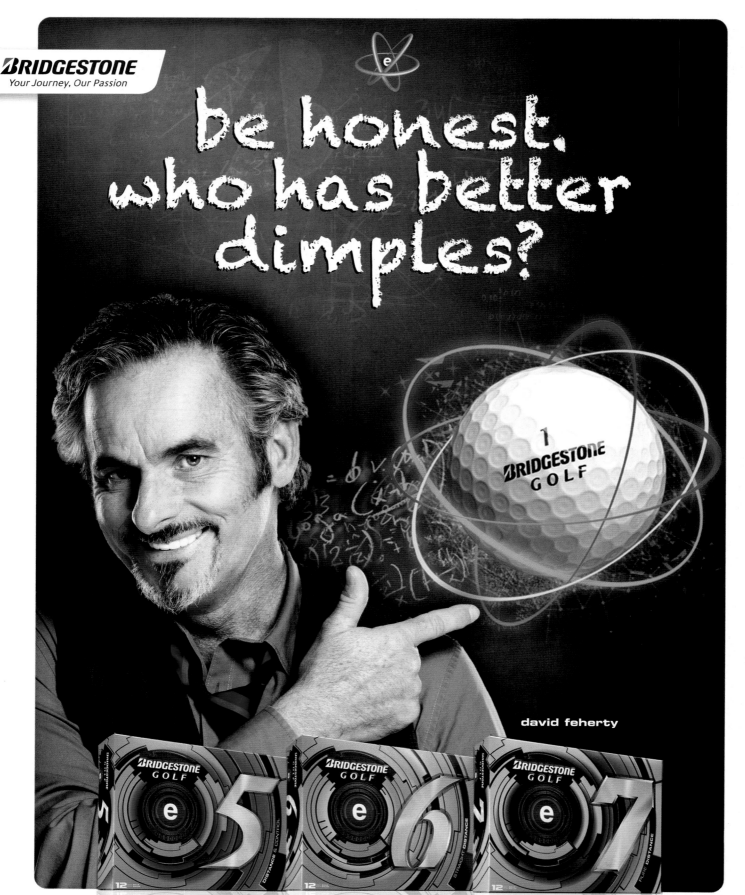

TAYLOR MADE
LETHAL | RRP: £28
http://taylormadegolf.eu

CALLAWAY
TOP | HEX CHROME | RRP: £35
BOTTOM | HEX HOT | RRP: £25
www.callawaygolf.com

PINNACLE
TOP | GOLD | RRP: £13
BOTTOM | BLING | RRP: £14
www.pinnaclegolf.com

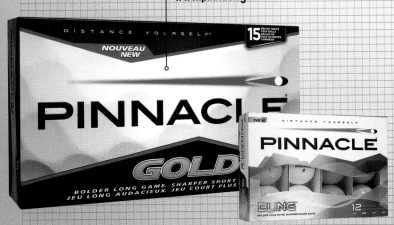

WILSON STAFF
TOP | FG TOUR X | RRP: £35
BOTTOM | DX2 SOFT | RRP: £18
www.wilson.com/en-gb/golf/

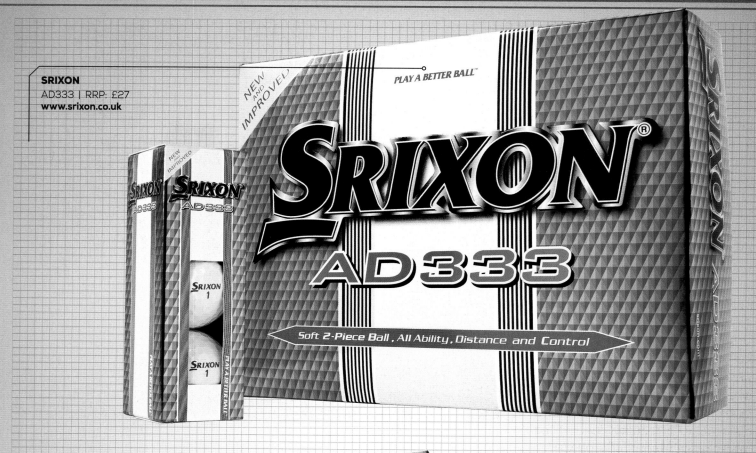

SRIXON

AD333 | RRP: £27
www.srixon.co.uk

SRIXON

SOFT FEEL | RRP: £26
www.srixon.co.uk

DESIRABLE DIMPLES

The 20XI will be the first **Nike** model on tour to use the company's RZN core technology, delivering greater distance and accuracy, while the One RZNx offers less spin for longer drives, but more spin around the greens. **Mizuno's** MP-S is the company's third generation ball, and 2013 see's it launched in the west for the first time. It provides tour performance with great distance and spin. The D201 is a great all round ball, suited to all handicaps, and is designed for superior stability. **Srixon's** fifth generation AD333 two piece ball aims to provide great all-round two piece ball perfomance. It delivers its best performance at club head speeds of over 80mph. The Soft Feel model gives the average golfer increased distance, with reduced spin off the driver aiming to provide straighter shots. The latest Lethal ball from **Taylor Made** features a five layer construction for increased spin and control, while **Callaway's** 2013 Hex balls (Hot and Chrome) feature hexagonal dimples for reduced drag and increased stability in flight, while the Chrome boasts an S-Tech core, for a softer feel. **Wilson Staff** claim its DX2 is the softest hitting ball on the market, and is the lowest compression ball available to golfers in the UK, making it ideal for all golfers (including juniors). The FG Tour X ball demonstrates tour characteristics, with great distance and exceptional spin. **Pinnacle's** Bling ball is great for those looking to make a statement on the course, while the company's Gold balls have been around for years, and in 2013 offer enahnced spin and distance.

NIKE
TOP | 20XI | RRP: £40
BOTTOM | ONE RZN X | RRP: £30
www.nikegolf.eu

MIZUNO
TOP | MP-S | RRP: £50
BOTTOM | D201 | RRP: £25
golf.mizunoeurope.com

It's not the taking part

1 SRIXON

It's the winning

year after **year** after **year** after **year** after **year** after **year**

2007   **2008**   **2009**   **2010**   **2011**   **2012**

At Srixon, we're all about the winning. So much so that winning golfers have made us the UK's top-selling 2-piece ball brand for the last six years in a row*. If the ball you're currently using isn't a Srixon, then quite simply you've yet to find the winning choice for you. Go to www.srixon.co.uk today to find the right ball for your game!

WANNA CHANGE YOUR GAME?
BETTER CHANGE YOUR BALLS!

SRIXON®
www.srixon.co.uk

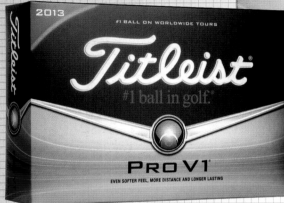

TITLEIST
TOP | PRO V1X | RRP: £51
BOTTOM | PRO V1 | RRP: £51
www.titleist.co.uk

Titleist's new Pro V1 range of balls aim to provide a softer feel for better spin and control, more distance and more durability than previous models. The Pro V1x is a higher launching ball, with lower spin for longer, straighter shots. These balls are ideally suited for your advanced player, and are the number one ball played on tour. **Bridgestone's** Tour B330-RX balls have dual dimple technology, which provide a shallow angle of descent for enhanced roll. The inside dimple is designed to provide extra thrust when striking the ball. The 'e' family of balls caters for all standard of golfer. The e5 offers great distance and control while the e7 is a pure distance ball.

BRIDGESTONE
TOP | E6 | RRP: £26
BOTTOM | TOUR B330-RX | RRP: £45
www.bridgestonegolf.com

DESIRABLE DIMPLES

The golf ball we know and love today has come a long way from its humble roots as a hand-crafted, goose feather stuffed sphere, and is now an aerodynamically perfect piece of precision engineering. A whole industry has sprung up since back in the 1600s, with hundreds of different manufacturers producing thousands of different balls, each with their own playing characteristics. Here are some of the best ones to look out for in 2013.

TITLEIST 913D2

RRP: £344
www.titleist.co.uk

LYNX BLACK CAT

RRP: £149
www.lynxgolf.co.uk

9.5

10.5

BOOM BOOM 2

HOT | TECHNOLOGY

Lynx

9°

"Driver technologies are becoming increasingly advanced, Lynx's Boom Boom 2 is a fine example"

LYNX BOOM BOOM 2

RRP: £349
www.lynxgolf.co.uk

6

"To be a good driver, you need to have the correct amount of clubhead speed - at least 80 mph"

7

Cobra's 2013 Amp Cell family of drivers offers everyone (from the beginner to the pro) plenty of options. Most clubs come in four colours, and feature six adjustable loft settings for easy customisation. The Amp Cell pro driver offers tour trajectory with a lower, more neutral centre of gravity. The new **Nike** Covert drivers offer a tour and game improvement option, and both feature adjustable loft options for greater club customisation. **Titleist's** 913D2 provides classic looks with exceptional distance and forgiveness, while a built in slight draw bias helps the ball curl in the air. The **Lynx** black cat is back, and still on fine form. The glare-proof 460cc head provides an extremely penatrative shot. Lynx's Boom Boom 2 driver comes with an inovative head cover that warms the driver's gas filled titanium head to its optimum temperature, providing greater length - a very advanced piece of kit.

"Manufacturers spread a club's weight around the head to make its sweet spot as large as possible"

IN THE DRIVING SEAT

1. **Ping Anser** | RRP: £355 | www.ping.com
2. **Cobra Amp Cell Pro** | RRP: £319 | www.cobragolf.com
3. **Ping i20** | RRP: £299 | www.ping.com
4. **Cobra Amp Cell** | RRP: £249 | www.cobragolf.com
5. **Ping G25** | RRP: £299 | www.ping.com
6. **Nike VR_S Covert** | RRP: £249 | www.nikegolf.eu
7. **Nike VR_S Covert Tour** | RRP: £349 | www.nikegolf.eu

> "A lighter head means a faster swing, which means greater power"

Hailing from their high value M1 package set, **Ben Sayer's** M1 driver offers excellent bang for your buck. As always, **Dunlop's** fantastic range of products are extremely well priced, and the 2013 NZ9 and DP1 only show that a lower price point can also offer high quality. **Taylor Made's** 2013 RBZ drivers use RocketBallz technology which provides faster ball speed and longer distances, while the company's R1 driver features three tuneable technologies. These are adjustable weights, lofts and a seven position face angle sole plate. **Wilson Staff's** new for 2013 D-100 is the lightest driver the manufacturer has ever produced, allowing for a faster swing. It also features a large sweet spot for more regular hitting. **Mizuno's** 2013 JPX825 is the company's most advanced driver yet. A five piece titanium construction design enables Mizuno to distribute weight around the driver head to provide straighter and longer hitting. **Ping's** 2013 i20 is a classically shaped head and features an optimised centre of gravity that reduces spin off the club head, offering the golfer enhanced penetration. The company's G25 is suited to all standards of golfer, and comes with trajectory tuning technology making it highly customisable. Along with the adjustable loft option, this club aims to improve your distance and accuracy. The same technology is featured in the Anser, but the latter boasts different cosmetics.

DRIVERS

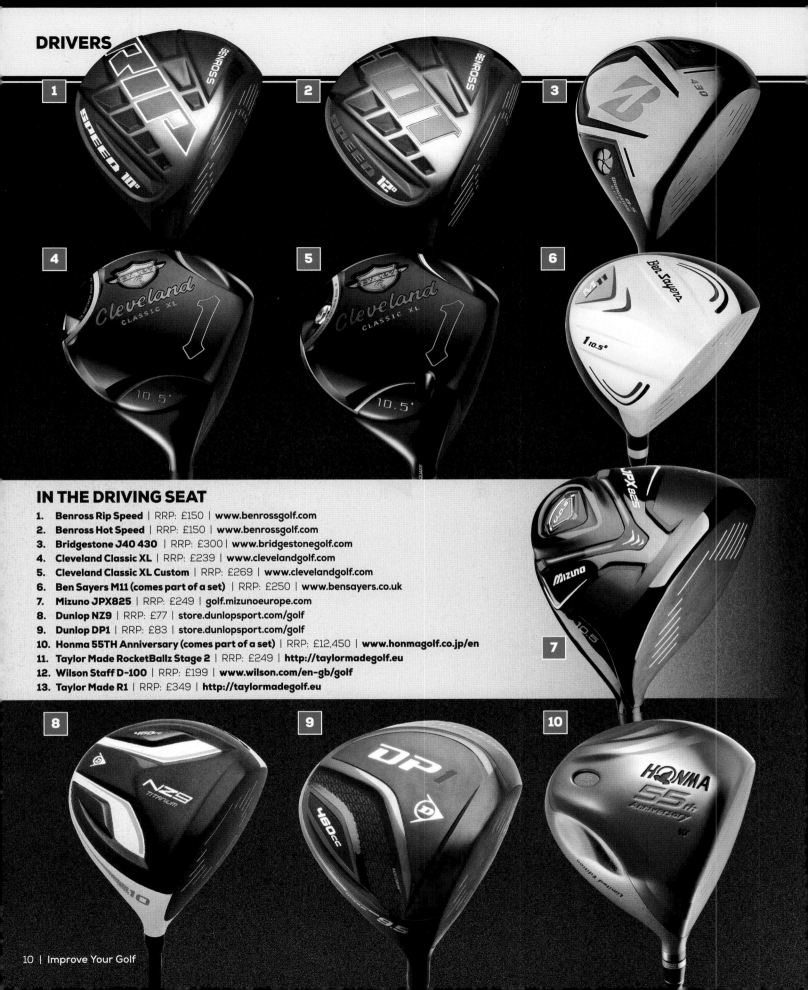

IN THE DRIVING SEAT

1. **Benross Rip Speed** | RRP: £150 | www.benrossgolf.com
2. **Benross Hot Speed** | RRP: £150 | www.benrossgolf.com
3. **Bridgestone J40 430** | RRP: £300 | www.bridgestonegolf.com
4. **Cleveland Classic XL** | RRP: £239 | www.clevelandgolf.com
5. **Cleveland Classic XL Custom** | RRP: £269 | www.clevelandgolf.com
6. **Ben Sayers M11 (comes part of a set)** | RRP: £250 | www.bensayers.co.uk
7. **Mizuno JPX825** | RRP: £249 | golf.mizunoeurope.com
8. **Dunlop NZ9** | RRP: £77 | store.dunlopsport.com/golf
9. **Dunlop DP1** | RRP: £83 | store.dunlopsport.com/golf
10. **Honma 55TH Anniversary (comes part of a set)** | RRP: £12,450 | **www.honmagolf.co.jp/en**
11. **Taylor Made RocketBallz Stage 2** | RRP: £249 | **http://taylormadegolf.eu**
12. **Wilson Staff D-100** | RRP: £199 | **www.wilson.com/en-gb/golf**
13. **Taylor Made R1** | RRP: £349 | **http://taylormadegolf.eu**

THE DRIVING SEAT

GO THE DISTANCE WITH 2013's HOTTEST DRIVING TALENT

Callaway's two new additions for 2013 both come with OptiFit. This hosel technology lets you adjust the club's face angle from open to closed, aiming to give you improved accuracy and trajectory. **Homna's** driver range for this year not only provides excellent performance with a touch of luxury, but you'll need a deep pocket to afford some of the priciest drivers on the market. **Benross'** 2013 range of Speed drivers (featured over the page) offer a stunning matte black finish. The Rip is designed for those after a long, low ballflight, while the Hot offers a little more forgiveness. **Bridgestone's** J40 430 favours the better player, and its improved face thickness offers enhanced stability. The Classic XL driver from **Cleveland** has the largest and deepest club face of any driver in golf while the XL Custom offers an adjustable hosel, similar to Callaway's, and a changebale weight port which gives you room to fine tune your setup.

HONMA TOUR WORLD TW717

RRP: £895
www.honmagolf.co.jp/en

CALLAWAY RAZR FIT XTREME

RRP: £329
www.callawaygolf.com

CALLAWAY X HOT

RRP: £279
www.callawaygolf.com

EQUIPMENT
GUIDE

YOU'RE ABOUT TO GET A WHOLE LOT LONGER.

YOU'RE WELCOME.

Introducing the XHot Family from Callaway. The new standard in distance from every
club in the bag and from every lie on the course. See how at callawaygolf.com/xhot

THE NEW STANDARD IN DISTANCE.

BRING.IT.ON.

EQUIPMENT GUIDE

74

8

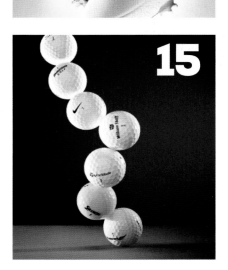

68

50

28

15

44

WELCOME

I expect you've picked up this MagBook because you want to sharpen up your golf skills. Aside from the PGA Pro tutorials you'll find if you turn this MagBook upside down and go to the front, it's fair to say that this section right here on golfing equipment is just as important in gaining that edge on your rivals.

In a lifetime, golfers of all levels invest in a serious amount of equipment. And as technology improves, whether that's in the form of clubs, balls, apparel, or perhaps gadgets, there's no doubt the sheer number of products available can be increasingly bewildering.

To address this matter, we're presenting you with the best offerings from some of the industry's finest manufacturers, ensuring that whenever you stand astride that first tee, you'll be prepared to win.

Danny Poulter, PGA Professional